# Pond Memories

## More Takes from a Wildlife Rehabilitator

## Lil Anderson

TURNSTONE 🐦 PRESS

Pond Memories: More Tales from a Wildlife Rehabilitator
copyright © Lil Anderson 2009

Turnstone Press
Artspace Building
206-100 Arthur Street
Winnipeg, MB
R3B 1H3 Canada
www.TurnstonePress.com

Turnstone Press gratefully acknowledges the assistance of the Canada Council for the Arts, the Manitoba Arts Council, the Government of Canada through the Canada Book Fund, and the Government of Manitoba through the Department of Culture, Heritage, Tourism and Sport, Arts Branch, for our publishing activities.

Cover design: Jamis Paulson
Interior design: Sharon Caseburg
Cover photo: Lil Anderson
Photos by: Lil Anderson
Illustrations by: Christine Kerrigan
Printed and bound in Canada by Friesens for Turnstone Press.

Library and Archives Canada Cataloguing in Publication

Anderson, Lil, 1956–
    Pond memories : more tales from a wildlife rehabilitator / Lil Anderson.

ISBN 978-0-88801-346-0

    1. Wildlife rehabilitation—Ontario—Kenora. 2. Anderson, Lil, 1956–.
1. Castors. I. Title.

SF996.45.A543 2009          639.97'937'092          C2009-905012-9

**Mixed Sources**
Cert no. SW-COC-001271
© 1996 FSC
FSC

# Pond Memories

*Also by Lil Anderson*

Beavers Eh to Bea

*To Bruce, with all my love.*

# Pond Memories

# Pond Memories

My breath curled back into my face, creating a thick fog on my glasses with each puff. Blurred vision made my progress slow and clumsy along the snow-packed trail the dogs and I followed.

The trail led out of the dense woods into a small clearing, with the field we sought just beyond that. As we approached the creek that rimmed the big field, an icy blast of wind converted the steam on my spectacles to a thick frost.

"Argggh," I snarled.

I peered over their frames, just in time to see a dark heap on the trail in front of me. I stumbled off the hard-packed trail into deep, loose snow as the mass formed a recognizable shape through my fogged lenses. Better to get a boot full of snow than to step on ol' Heidi, who had taken a time out to lie in the middle of the trail to remove the icy buildup from her feet.

Slowly and methodically, the old dog gnawed each golf-ball-sized hunk of ice from her pads. As each icy ball was ripped off, she would spit it into the snow, "thwip," before turning to the next foot. The cold seeped into my joints, as I impatiently shuffled from foot to foot, watching her while she attended to her task. The last paw held a larger, more tenacious hitchhiker.

She gnawed for a few more seconds, then, sensing my impatience, viciously yanked off the offending clump, hair and all. "Thwip." This hirsute toe-ball joined the others in the deep snow. As I watched the fuzzy brown lump disappear into the grey depths, I fantasized some poor owl spending a fruitless night staring through the snow at the hairy chunk, waiting for this strange-looking mouse to move.

After she had made a few feeble, unsuccessful attempts to stand, I slipped my hand under Heidi's hips and gently lifted her to her feet. She grinned back apologetically before loping awkwardly down the trail in front of me. Poor Heidi; I was afraid my old friend was feeling her age. A smaller, brown-and-white blur streaked by us, slowing down only slightly as she ripped off an icy toe-ball herself. Brill was just too busy to lie down while removing these annoying chunks. She had mastered a technique of grabbing on to the ice lump mid-stride and ripping it off with her teeth without breaking pace, and only occasionally tripping herself up in the process. There was simply too much for her to sniff and explore in the wondrous outdoors to bother slowing down for such petty and annoying cling-ons.

Although they were both Wachtelhunds or more commonly, Wachtels, a breed of German hunting dogs, Brill and Heidi couldn't have been more different in personality. Both were extremely intelligent, but Heidi had almost a human psyche while Brill was just a really, really smart dog. Heidi and I had been through a lot together and she was a good friend and companion. As I watched her struggle valiantly in the loose snow, my vision blurred again.

"Darned condensation," I sniffed.

While we waited for Brill to come out from the woods, where she was busily sorting out fresh hare scents, Heidi and I stood in the bright winter sun, both of us staring dreamily across the snow- and ice-covered beaver pond.

"Things sure have changed, haven't they, old girl?" I said.

Even though I was pretty sure she was getting deaf now, she turned and looked at me inquisitively.

"Still reading my mind, are you?"

She sniffed, grinned and lurched up onto all fours again and initiated the trek back to the house.

Things really had changed since we first took our new pup, Heidi, for a walk across this big field. We may have even been trespassing a little bit back then. The property had been for sale for a long time, and my husband

Bruce and I wantonly eyed it, daring to dream it might someday be ours. Back a decade or so, when I started out as a novice backyard rehabilitator, I discovered that this land with its large field was perfect for testing the wings of some of the raptors I had in my care. None of the present-day restrictions for releasing wildlife were in place at that time, so when I had a hawk or owl ready to release to the wild, I could bring it out to these old fields to test fly. If they flew strong and steady, I released them to the field, where they could start their new chance at life in this productive, suitable habitat. Adult birds of

prey retain memories of their previously held territories and could eventually return to try to reclaim them, or, if the released bird was young and still trying to find a place to call its own, it could choose to remain in the area. Voles and mice abounded in the sedge meadow and field, providing lots of food for the hawks and owls while they strengthened their wings and honed newly developed hunting skills.

At the edge of the field, an old log house, constructed with the dovetailed joints popular in its era, stood, restored from the ruinous state we had found it in. Built sometime in the early 1900s, it held a mysterious history; some said it was a bootlegger's homestead, others that he was just an old farmer. Judging by the mountains of old, empty, green wine bottles we keep unearthing around the property, I think the former was true. The bottom logs of the old house had rotted and collapsed down into an old dirt cellar, but there was still plenty of the original place sturdy enough that we felt it could be restored, and even be habitable in a pinch.

The biggest change in our landscape since those days, though, was the frozen beaver pond that the dogs and I were walking beside. What had been a mossy, sedge-covered depression ringed with willows and alders when Bruce and I first visited this property was now an impressive, vital new pond. When we started building our house on our newly acquired land, we had a small, furry houseguest that also needed a place to live. An orphaned beaver in my care, Eh, had spent the winter prior to our building on this land down in the basement of our house in the city. When we started building our new house, I believed that he was finally old enough, big enough and independent enough to be released to the wild. We thought the small lake on our property would be perfect, as there was plenty of food and a colony of beavers on one end and an empty beaver house for him to squat in on the other.

Best of all, we could check on him from time to time, as the lake was small enough to see or hear him no matter which end he was at. But our plans were foiled when the resident beavers took offence to this newcomer, and Eh was viciously attacked. Fortunately, we checked up on him before his wounds became too infected. When I saw the severity of the cuts and lacerations on his back, I knew we had to bring him home to mend. Once he healed, we would have to figure out a new location for his release, a place of his own where he could learn to be a wild beaver, but where wild beavers wouldn't challenge him until he had learned proper beaver etiquette.

A few weeks later, when Eh's injuries had healed, Bruce and I had a discussion about what would look better in front of our house—a grassy, lumpy, tick-infested meadow, or a nice shimmering new pond? All options considered, the pond won out. A backhoe operator on-site had just finished carving out the basement for our new house and was preparing to load his machine onto a flatbed truck when we approached him. He looked at us rather strangely when we directed him to the meadow and told him what we wanted. "You say you are doing this for a *beaver*?" He shook his head incredulously, but went about the task of excavating a deep depression in the heavy clay soils. I'm pretty sure we were the topic of conversation at a few coffee breaks for some time after that.

This newly excavated feature would become an important addition to our landscape once it eventually filled with water. It presented us with a new habitat type, a ready-made nursery area for young animals, and provided us with a magnificent vista and incredible viewing and photographic opportunities.

Eh had spent that first long, lonely winter in a makeshift beaver house, and when he emerged from the icy pond the next spring, he was a changed beaver... that is, he actually acted like a beaver. A wild female soon joined Eh in the pond and the two of them redesigned the ever-increasing water body to their own specifications. Eh moved on after spending a few years in the pond with his mate and fathering some ten or eleven kits during his stay.

Another orphaned beaver, Cameron, replaced Eh in my heart and my home and currently lives in the pond with some of Eh's offspring. On this particular cold day, it was Cameron and his kin who slept and passed time in whatever manner beavers do under the snow and ice, safe in the warmth and darkness of their lodge. Heidi and I lumbered up the last stretch of the trail towards the house, as Brill bounded across the ice to the large beaver lodge at the edge of the pond, racing to its peak. She paused momentarily to grin happily at us, before barking down the steaming vent at the top of the house, no doubt waking the occupants from their daytime nap.

"Cameron is going to get you when he comes out this spring, Brill!" I called.

Her response to my warning was to growl playfully, rip a peeled, greyed aspen pole out of the frozen mud on the house and drag it across the pond to where I stood.

"No, I can't throw that, it weighs a ton," I scolded, "and, Heidi wants to go home. She's old and she's cold. And quit wrecking Cameron's lodge."

We passed a dense tangle of alder and balsam along the trail, and both dogs glanced anxiously into the thicket and growled. They quickened their pace until we were well down the trail.

"What good memories these dogs have," I thought.

The tangle they eyed so suspiciously had once concealed an angry moose calf that exploded out of the darkness to attack them. The calf had only responded to a natural fear of canids when it came barrelling out of the bushes to confront the dogs. But it definitely had made us all uneasy that day, giving the dogs scary memories of that spot. Memories of my days as a moose's mother came flooding back.

# A Little Bull Goes a Long Way

"Hi, Lil, it's Andy." The voice on the telephone was only too familiar. Andy, a conservation officer in Sioux Lookout, Ontario, is often the recipient of injured or orphaned wildlife from that remote area. Since Andy called me at home, I knew it must be on behalf of some furred or feathered critter.

Now, if I recollect Andy's account of the dilemma correctly, it went something like this. It seemed that anglers, fishing the waters of Lac Seul in the Sioux Lookout district on the opening weekend of walleye season, were blessed with the unique opportunity to watch a cow moose swimming with her two calves from a small island to the mainland.

Moose sometimes seek out these little windswept island habitats to bear their young, because they are relatively safe from bears and wolves and biting insects. Once the calf or calves are strong enough, mom leads them to the protection of thicker forests and the plentiful foods of the mainland. Often these calving islands have only a few shrubs and trees on them—young moose don't need much except mom when suckling—and while a moose may feel secure from the four-legged predators, a boat of humans intruding into her space is different. She may feel compelled to move her young before they have gained enough strength to swim to shore.

Whatever the full details of the situation were, it seemed that the anglers followed the cow and calves, happily capturing the moment on film and from the safety of their boat. In their excitement they didn't notice that one calf panicked as it was swamped by the boat's wake. He swallowed and inhaled water, and then flailed helplessly, trying to stay above water. The cow took the other calf and ran up on shore into the dense brush. The panicked calf, weak and half-drowned, couldn't climb the steep bank where the cow had been forced to shore. Giving up, he lay down and bawled for mom. Had the cow been given the chance to pick her spot to climb out of the water, she would likely have chosen a low shoreline, easy for her calves' tiny legs to traverse. But the boat had scared her into picking a less than suitable spot, which had caused a crisis for the one calf.

The anxious and repentant anglers stayed on shore with the calf, worrying about its fate, while their scent and sounds drove the cow even further away. They decided they couldn't just leave it lying there bawling, so they gave up their fishing for the day and delivered the weakened calf to the Sioux Lookout Ministry of Natural Resources office.

Hence the telephone call from Andy.

After I agreed to take in the calf, we had to work out an arrangement to deliver the calf to me in Kenora within a few days. I was not in a position to pick it up myself any earlier. I wasn't holding out much hope for its chances of survival, as this was a newborn ungulate, with little or no substantive food in it. In addition, it sounded like it might have developed pneumonia, most likely from inhaling water during its panicked swim through the boat's wake.

Andy's wife Penny joined the rescue attempt once she heard of the calf's plight. Over the telephone we discussed the best way to give the little fellow a chance at life. Penny wasn't feeling all that well, battling with illness herself, and this endeavour would take a lot of energy. But knowing of Penny's nursing experience, I felt better, and thought that the calf might have a chance of survival. Penny was even able to convince a friend of hers into donating a supply of goat's milk, which is easily digested by young animals. Now this may not seem extraordinary, but the small northern community of Sioux Lookout is not known for agricultural animals. To have a ready supply of fresh goat's milk was a godsend to me, and made me feel the task ahead was surmountable.

Penny warmed the calf and fed it, but she was concerned with the rattling, wet sounds the little animal made as it struggled to breathe. Over the telephone, she described the calf's bluish-coloured gums, a sign we both realized as serious. She gave it an injection of antibiotics to help combat its pneumonia, a desperate measure. But we had no choice, even though we knew with ungulates, particularly in babes, the antibiotics themselves can cause problems in their digestive system. We had to try to treat his condition. Problem was, the calf needed every bit of natural bacteria he had in his tiny little tummy to help him digest food and gain strength.

As we had feared, within a short time the antibiotics caused severe diarrhea, further sapping his strength. We now had a very desperate situation on our hands.

Penny stabilized the calf to a state in which we thought it was strong enough to transport to Kenora. The responsibility would then be in my hands to do what I could for him.

Penny was also able to convince her goat-keeper friends to continue to supply me with milk once I received the calf. Not only that, she also persuaded, without much difficulty, Bearskin Airways, which serves the remote communities of the region, to deliver the milk to me on a regular basis. I had been unable to find a source of fresh goat's milk in my hometown on such short notice. Often even the powdered form is hard to find in the supermarkets in Kenora, and is very expensive. If the calf's condition stabilized, I could later switch it to a more economical, readily available and easily digested calf starter. It had been recommended to me as a suitable food for moose calves in captivity. But that would be later, if all else went well. Adding new foods at this point would only make his diarrhea worse.

When Andy delivered the calf to me, I was dismayed by what I saw. The little animal was very quiet and its mental and physical state was weak. As Andy prepared to leave for the long drive home, I promised to keep Penny and him updated on the calf's progress. I was worried I would have bad news for them too soon, maybe even before Andy made it home. Grimly, I grabbed my wheelbarrow and wheeled the large dog kennel containing the sick little animal down to the old log house. He had to be kept very warm, dry, and quiet, and the old building seemed to be a perfect place to house him for now. When I reached our destination, I opened the kennel door and a subdued, sick little moose calf reluctantly uncurled from his fetal position, stood, shook half-heartedly, and wobbled out. As he stood there with his head hanging, I knew he was very ill. Any healthy calf would immediately be sniffing, bellowing, and exploring its surroundings. This little guy didn't even want to move until I led him to his new bed, where he sniffed the fresh straw lackadaisically. Without more ado, he plopped down with a groan, closing his eyes. I left him to rest while I went back to the house to warm the goat's milk Penny had sent with him, not entirely convinced he would be alive when I returned.

I walked back to where I had left the calf, happy to see he was indeed still alive. When I held the bottle to him he was quite eager to take this replacer milk. Although he struggled to breathe, he took readily to the bottle, thanks largely to Penny's patience and gentleness in introducing him to this unfamiliar feeding device. In past cases, I have found that if orphans have bad experiences with bottle-feeding they starve themselves rather than accept the feeding. Unfocused, untrained force-feeding of a young animal can be bad news. Inexperienced caregivers, wanting only to help a frightened, vocalizing baby animal, might squirt cold, unfamiliar fluids down into the throat and lungs of their wards. Or they may wedge the bottle forcefully into the youngster's tender mouth, causing cuts, scrapes, and sores. Human children, too young to understand proper care, loud in their own excitement and impatient to succeed, might be allowed to feed a little beast. Any of these situations are contrary to producing a feeling of safety in a young animal, and can easily turn it away from the easiest method of saving it from starvation.

Animals, young or old, will hesitate to feed when stressed, nervous, or scared. After all, survival in the wild often depends on quick flight. And one can't flee quickly or comfortably on a full stomach. Natural fight-or-flight conditions also occur in the body, directing blood flow to legs and lungs, and away from the digestive system. Sometimes the digestive system will empty itself, to lighten the load. Needless to say, if an animal is overly stressed and scared, it's not a good time to try to feed it. Every sense of survival it has will direct it to reject the food. But to this calf, the bottle was his friend. Penny had done well.

Once the little calf was warm and fed, he seemed to gain a bit of strength. Now, I had to deal with the rattle and racking cough that shook his frame. His gums were still a bluish hue, a bad sign. There was a very bad smell to his breath, coming from deep down. Could his lungs have become gangrenous so soon after inhaling the lake water? Again, I feared that saving this patient was a lost cause.

I remembered seeing parents of children with lung and respiratory disease "thump" their kids' ribs in a certain way to expel built-up fluids and phlegm. I have even "thumped" my own rib cage when I've had an asthma attack or bronchitis in order to loosen the congested material. It sure couldn't hurt to try the procedure on this little moose calf. I knew if I didn't do something and do it quickly, it would die.

First, I reached under the calf's chest and laid my left arm up along the base of the rib cage, with my hand under its thin brisket. With the flat palm of my right hand, I started a slow, gentle thumping, starting from the back and working to the front of the rib cage, stopping when I could no longer hear a hollow sound and no breath puffed from his nostrils. Then I would start again, slow but steady, back to front. The calf stood there, obviously scared, with its head hanging low, and its soft brown eyes half-closed, dull and lifeless. Little puffs of air escaped from his runny little nostrils at each thump. When I started thumping the opposite side of his chest, the rattling of his breathing sounded very loose and wet. I wasn't sure if that were a good sign or a very bad sign, until he coughed and then coughed again. With that second cough, he expelled a large fetid plug of phlegm and mucus and copious amounts of thin fluids, the cause of the rattling in his breathing. After I wiped away the crud from his mouth and nose, he drew a few deep, decidedly quieter breaths, and I swear I saw a look of relief in his soft brown eyes, which were now wide open.

After that, he seemed to get stronger by the moment. Soon he was taking deep breaths as if he smelled something wonderful that he could just not get enough of. He wandered around me for a few minutes, showing interest in his surroundings, before flopping down exhausted. The poor thing deserved a rest, so I left him bedded down in the warm sun while I went about my chores. I kept glancing covertly to the field where he lay, to make sure he was safe and still holding his head up. A few hours later, when I went to feed him again and move him into the old house for the evening, his gums had turned pink. He held his head up, he was interested in his surroundings, and he was hungry. He no longer stopped after a few sucks of the bottle to breathe, he now downed it in a steady draw, caving the sides of the two-litre plastic bottle in his urgency. He was on the mend from that point on.

When I realized the worst was maybe over, I called Penny to let her know what had happened. She was ecstatic, as were Andy and their young sons, all of whom had grown fond of the calf during their short acquaintance. One of their sons had asked if I would call him by the name they gave him, and I agreed. I wrote the name "Brownie" on his record, in acknowledgment of the great job their mom had done for the calf. Call me superstitious and call me unprofessional, but naming an animal seems to give it strength, character, and something to grow into.

The calf responded as all babies do after a feeding: he had to go to the bathroom. This became a pattern. Every day, I fed him in solitude and shade near the edge of a small creek that fed into the beaver pond. Once finished with his bottle, he would wander off to tend to his toilet as I gathered up the feeding dishes. I was constantly amazed when this tiny calf would instinctively wobble into the water, assuming a distinctive squat over the creek. Even at this tender age, the instinct to hide the scent of his bodily fluids from possible predators was strong. Once he discovered the creek, he would urinate and defecate into its flowing water whenever the need arose.

When tending to young animals in my care, I allow them time and freedom to explore their surroundings at their own speed. This way, I spend a lot of enjoyable time observing their actions in this natural environment and learn from them. Sometimes my observations can seem rather absurd, albeit insightful. One day while watching the calf assume a strange squat position as he performed his toilet over the stream, I realized his stance reminded me of some other animal, but which? Then a telephone conversation I had a few years back came to mind.

"Lil," the caller said, "I know this sounds crazy, but do you know if there are any kangaroos running loose? You know, maybe one escaped or something?"

I assured her that I had not heard of any such thing, but asked why she was inquiring. She went on to say that while driving the Trans-Canada Highway, she had seen a small brown animal which from the back looked just like a kangaroo: long ears, long back, and a squat stance. The part she found odd was that it was near a cow moose feeding along the roadside. I'm sure she had been looking at what I was seeing now... a small, brown, long-eared animal, assuming a frog-like position that didn't look anything like a moose, but could with just a bit of imagination, be mistaken for a tailless 'roo.

Within days of his lungs clearing, the calf was running and playing in the waters of the pond, splashing, kicking, and snorting. He still had serious bouts of diarrhea, which concerned me, but he was able to take care of that messy problem with his own hooves.

One morning while I cleaned up after his feeding, I watched as he started sniffing the bank of the creek with great interest. He pawed tentatively at the slope until shiny grey clay was exposed. He first started to lick and chew at the clay, which stuck to the tips of his hooves, and then he took bites from the ground. After ingesting a considerable amount of the exposed clay, he moved on to the rotting leaves and sedges that had collected at the edge of the stream. He was frantic and excited as he sought out the soggiest material, consuming it without hesitation. His diarrhea was pretty much gone by the end of that day. I concluded that the soils and clays must have held the probiotics and minerals his digestive system needed to function properly, and somehow he was hardwired to know this. We buy a commercial product made from kaolin clay to take care of our human digestive ailments. The little moose just cut back on the excess processing and packaging.

I remembered that Beeper, a fawn I had raised a few years back, had sought out earth and decaying material for his diet as well. Organisms that break down the cellulose in leaf litter help herbivores digest their fibrous foods. Not only was the consumption of decaying material necessary, I realized that geophagy, or the eating of soil, was important to the survival of young animals, too. These facts are now well accepted by wildlife rehabilitators across the continent.

Renecker and Schwartz, in *Food Habits and Feeding Behaviour, Ecology and Management of North American Moose*, describe a muscular esophageal groove, which allows milk to bypass the three undeveloped fermentation chambers in the suckling ungulate's stomach and go straight to its well-developed abomasums, or stomach. As a calf grows, and ingested bacteria flourish in the rumen, it is able to digest and get nutrient from forage. I assume the soggy, decomposing materials Brownie ate helped the rumen develop into functioning chambers and ended his digestive disorder.

As charming as Brownie could be, he was definitely a little bull bent on challenging the world. The wood frogs were congregating along the same stream that the calf frequented. They were at the peak of their breeding season, and were active day and night, sometimes in large groups. Often, in the middle of these masses of legs and eyes, there would be only a single female, but that didn't seem to discourage the amorous male frogs. But their squirmy, bobbing mass did make them quite obvious to Brownie's suspicious eye. I was unable to stop him from stomping on some of the hapless, preoccupied amphibians he decided were his enemies and had to be destroyed.

The little calf needed to be kept warm and dry, yet still allowed to act like a baby moose, which meant I had to soon find habitation other than the old log house that could provide these qualities of life for him. My wildlife rehabilitation structures and pens provided safe haven for small mammals and birds of prey, but none were suited for a moose calf.

I asked co-workers at the Ministry of Natural Resources and peers dealing with wildlife if they had any suggestions for such an enclosure. By a great stroke of luck it happened that the local sportsman groups and the Ontario Ministry of Natural Resources were participating in an elk reintroduction program. After the committee had constructed the temporary holding pen for the newly arrived elk, they had materials left over, which they generously donated to my rehabilitation centre. I, too, could now build my own ungulate enclosure, albeit on a smaller scale. An additional source of canvas donated by other friends ensured my enclosure could grow with the calf. And since Bruce had been instrumental in the planning of the elk recovery program from start to finish, he even had prior experience with pen building. What more could I ask?

This matting material, which is used when pulpwood fibre is milled into newsprint, made for excellent walls. It was soft and pliable, yet strong enough to prevent bears or wolves from tearing it. Bruce and I wrapped it around several trees to form a small, soft-walled compound. Within the rounded, shaped walls, we were able to enclose several aspen, white birch, and a small clump of beaked hazel and red osier dogwood. When the compound was finished, the walls were about ten feet tall and the enclosed area was about thirty feet across, on a gently sloped hillside facing the beaver pond. This let the sun shine into the enclosure, warming the ground during the day and, if it rained, ensured adequate drainage. Because of the trees, the calf could sun himself as he pleased, or lie in the shade.

At night, or if I was away from the house more than a few hours, or if it was rainy and cold, I moved him back to the safety of the room in the old log house. I had fixed up this room with a plastic-lined floor, and, to ensure he would have secure footing, I covered the plastic with felt matting and straw.

The old house provided added protection from the bears that might wander the edge of the pond in early morning and evenings. But it wasn't ideal, since moose do not belong in buildings, so as he got stronger, I put him in only when the weather was really nasty.

There were many times, though, that the weather was indeed really nasty. The intensity of the season's electrical storms was the talk of the town. The rumbles of each thunderclap rolled on and on across black, menacing skies, often lasting for hours. Early one morning a particularly eerie and ominous storm moved in, hitting our home with a vengeance. I had a hunch that it was going to be a big event when both dogs crawled from the foot of the bed up to my pillow, and started panting into my face. Brill was always spooked when thunderstorms rolled in, but old Heidi never seemed to mind too much— except this time! When I reached out into the darkness to pat and soothe the dogs, a long blue spark shot from my fingertips and zapped them, as the air was supercharged with static electricity. They did not find me to be much of a calming influence, and nervously moved away from me.

Bruce and I slept restlessly ourselves until an incredible flash, a deafening snap, and a clap of thunder caused us to bolt to a sitting position. Then, the clatter of an object crashing to the floor made us leap out of bed. In the flickering glow of the storm's light, I could see the small brass plaque with a bronzed elk head lying where it had landed after flying across the length of the bedroom. I was shaking like a leaf when I picked it up to examine it closely. In the now pulsing light of the storm, I could see that a link in the chain had melted into a blob. Somehow, the lighting strike had singled out this metal item, through the wall of the house.

After settling the dogs into the closet, where they huddled together for support, their eyes bulging in fear, and after being assured by Bruce that no house fire had been started by the strike, I, too, went back to bed. Sheer exhaustion allowed me to drift off, only to be reawakened by a painfully bright light shining in my eyes.

Now, without my glasses, I'm really blind, but I could make out a round ball of light floating past the bedroom window. I was sure I had imagined it, until a second, smaller light floated by. I stuck on my glasses and went out to the balcony. Drifting across the field, bouncing along the beaver pond and rolling down trees felled along its edge, were large fiery balls of intense greenish-yellow light. I could count at least a dozen of these Chernobyl-sized fireflies. I called Bruce, but by the time he woke and stumbled to the window, they were gone. I figured I must have been seeing things, dreaming perhaps, and I think he thought so, too.

My sanity was tested and found sound (or maybe the condition was hereditary), when I spoke with my mother the next morning. Some ten miles away, she also woke to bright lights and dogs barking. She went to investigate, only to see balls of light floating along the power lines and about six feet off the ground. Her luminescent visitors were also the size of pie plates, similar to mine. My brother, living on the same property, had one such fireball enter his house via a hydro line and into his breaker box, before it fizzled out. When I spoke of the event to my co-workers, one who lived about five miles away reported seeing the same thing at about the same time of night.

I assumed this was maybe "ball lightning" or perhaps, as a meteorologist I contacted the following week suggested, a phenomenon called "earth lights." However, while nothing I read described ball lightning floating free as these did, or covering such a large geographic area, it would seem that the properties of ball lightning are poorly understood, with some scientists even doubting its existence. The limited information I discovered when I researched "earth lights" more closely described what we had seen, but earth lights seem to be associated with fault lines in the earth, which aren't found in this area. Exactly what we saw remains a mystery, but the conditions must have been perfect, and the electrical charge in the region must have been so extensive that it covered an area large enough to include our property and those of my co-worker and my mother.

I found the occurrence of the strange lightning and the lightning strike on the house very unnerving. Fortunately, nothing untoward had happened to Brownie or any of the other animals in care. The next evening, when I went to herd Brownie to the safety of the old house, I was agitated and pushy as I kept my eye on yet another approaching storm. There was an eerie green glow that the sky sometimes develops, indicating the storm would be an intense one when it hit.

But Brownie had his own agenda, and when I took him away from the pen and began to walk him to the safety of the old house, the little moose wanted to feed and play, quite enjoying the low light of dusk. The strange lighting did make for good photography, so as I tried to convince the calf to venture down the narrow and rutted road to the old house, I used the opportunity to take pictures of him as he played, browsed, and dawdled. Through the camera's viewfinder, I watched as the calf turned into what looked like a big brown dandelion seed head, ready to blow apart in the wind.

Hmmm, how did he do that? I thought, as I watched his hair stand on end and then felt the hair on my own head and neck rise, as if I were touching a Van de Graaff generator.

I realized what was about to happen.

I dived into the flooded ditch, camera and all, as the calf darted into the woods. There was a flash of light and an air-shattering crack left my ears ringing painfully. Light spots danced in front of my eyes and my nostrils burned. But I was alive, albeit wet, muddy, and bruised. The lightning bolt had hit the transformer on the hydro pole in the driveway, some sixty feet away. Huffing and puffing at the strong smell of ozone in the air, the calf dashed back out of the woods, eyes bulging in fear as he raced ahead of me to the safety of the little house. He seemed more than willing to hide out there for the night after that scare.

This close call, following on the heels of the previous night's incident, left me for some time afterwards uncharacteristically anxious when I had to work outside if a storm was imminent. Unfortunately, my wards felt this in me and reacted accordingly, sometimes making it harder for me to care for them.

Later that week, Bruce and I found the reason for the flying elk plaque. A long furrow a foot or more deep was gouged in the earth from the base of a large scorched and splintered spruce tree. The furrow continued out into the field, ripped into the sod of the field down into the wet sedge meadow and up onto our lawn. It fizzled out in the lawn in a direct line to the spot on the wall where the plaque had hung. The wall of the house must have caught the end of the lightning bolt, like a whip, and there was just enough power left in it to melt the weak chain.

In the short time we had lived in our house, our immediate property, telephone and hydro lines had been struck many, many times by lightning. Fax machines, televisions, answering machines, and several other electronic devices met an early death. It seems we had moved into a storm corridor. Or maybe log homes are to lightning what trailer parks are to tornados. Eventually, we installed lightning rods, which reduce or redirect the electrical charge held in the ground, and as a result, we no longer seem to suffer from the numerous lightning strikes like we used to.

As Brownie grew, the calf's need for exercise also increased. When I let him out of the compound or old house, wherever he had spent the night, he would start doing laps around the field, pausing for a quick "creek stop" before racing off again. He took great joy in running past me while almost always directing a well-placed kick at my knee. Moose depend on their hooves and strong legs when defending themselves from bears or wolves, or even when fighting with one another during the mating season. This young bull was practicing for the day when he would meet the first love of his life.

I guess his mom may have put up with this practice if it were her lower legs being kicked, as hers were mainly large, dense bone with thick hide and very little flesh below the knees, but my sensitive, puny little extremities couldn't handle the sharp hoof edges and strength of his kick. I ended up having to carry a walking stick, which I would hold out from my side as he raced past. He was deadly in his aim and could send that stick flying some distance if he connected just so.

Sometimes, after his feeding and exercise, he would become quiet and aloof. If I weren't paying attention, I lost track of his whereabouts, as he would sneak off to find a secluded location to sleep. When he lay down, he seemed instinctively to find spots where, in the dappled light of the forest, he was almost invisible. But, if he chose the edge of the beaver pond to bed, the beavers, ever patrolling the pond for intruders, would give away his position. They would line up in front of his chosen position to glare at him, looking very much like fat exclamation marks on the still water.

Once he settled down, he did not come back to the compound until his next feeding was due, so I could leave and go about my other tasks. I suppose this is what his mom would have done as well, but she likely remained within the range of smell and sound, vigilant in the protection of her calf. After one feeding, he had melted away into the forest, so I took the opportunity to tend to my neglected garden. As I knelt to weed the rows, I heard cracking branches, a rushing sound, and felt a strange vibration in the ground. I looked up in time to see this small but determined little moose thundering out of the bushes at me, ears back and gums bared (his teeth were still insignificant). He

reared up on his back legs and flailed at me with his forty pounds or so of baby flesh. I believe he was responding to what our friend, Vince, refers to as the "predator pose," a position I had assumed by being on my hands and knees. I quickly stood to protect myself from his angry attack and he seemed confused, as the four-legged predator had disappeared. Snorting defiantly, he trotted proudly back to the cover of the trees, confident he had saved himself and his foster mom from a four-legged foe.

Dr. Vince Crichton (known fondly in the world of moose experts and the public as "Doc Moose") has spent a good portion of his life walking, talking, and living with moose in Canada's boreal zone and some non-boreal areas. He once told Bruce and me that the only time he was actually attacked was when he was filming a cow with a newborn young. The filming went fine, until he stepped off a hummock into a predator pose position to film the calf starting to nurse. The cow had tolerated his presence until this point, but went ballistic when she saw Vince, now hunched over and looking too much like a four-legged predator. Poor Vince almost met the same fate in that Manitoba bog as the wood frogs in my creek. Over the course of time that he was with us, I made every effort to ensure that the dogs were never in contact with the calf. Much to their chagrin, if the calf wasn't in the compound, they were confined to the house under my direct supervision. It wasn't that I was worried that they would start chasing the calf, as they adhere to the "No, that's Mom's" command and will leave even the most tempting visitor alone. It just is bad practice to make the calf think dogs are his friends, and vice versa.

One day while I was away at work, Brownie managed to squeeze out of his compound. After fruitlessly searching the field for me with my omnipresent food supply, he had blended back into the woods to hide or browse. When I came home, I wanted to give the dogs a good long walk and some loving attention before tending to the calf and the other wards. I didn't want them feeling neglected and jealous because my attentions were focused elsewhere. I intended to give the calf his supper when the dogs were safely returned to the house, assuming he was sleeping in the compound where I had left him that morning. As we walked the path back of the old field, young Brill was the first to show signs that something was wrong, looking over her shoulder nervously. Then Heidi stopped, swung up her head, and started a low growl in her throat. She stood up on her hind legs and stared into the brush.

This is not a good sign, I said to myself, as this is how she reacts when she is hunting big game, not like most hunting dogs, who run, bark, and chase their quarry. Having scented or sensed an animal, she would stand and focus on it until I too could see the object of her attention. So I peered along the line her nose had assumed to see what had her concerned this time. From the loud crashing in the brush, I knew whatever it was was close and getting closer fast.

Oh geez, I hope it's not a bear! I thought.

Suddenly, a small brown object, not much larger than Heidi, hurtled out of the alders. This thing had an evil look in its eyes. They were rolled back with only the whites showing, looking as only an angry moose can look, except a smaller version. The little bull must have thought that the strange dogs were attacking his surrogate mom, me. Their canid scent twigged some innate fear in him, and caused him to respond. And respond he did!

Brill knew that she shouldn't fight with any of Mom's special visitors. But she also knew enough to save herself and quickly dived under a tangled pile of alder trunks and branches. The little moose flailed away, breaking apart her flimsy fortress with his little hooves, until he realized that I was standing nearby. I had managed to scoot Heidi into the protection of thick brush out of his sight. I made a mewing sound, imitating a cow's contact call, to distract him from Brill. I had been using this call when interacting with the calf in the past, and thankfully, he responded. Brownie came to my side, eyes still rolling and flanks heaving, finally willing to let me lead him away.

The dogs were starting to ease themselves out of their hiding spots, but I quickly put them into the "sit, stay" mode with a hand signal. They responded quietly and obediently, slinking back out of sight without drawing the calf's attention. When I walked the calf back to the compound, I noticed his heart was pounding as hard as mine, but I'm sure the dogs had us both beat. I settled the calf into the compound, and repaired the opening he had escaped through. Once done, I walked back to the edge of the field and called for the dogs. Two relieved-looking Wachtels slunk down the trail towards me, eyes like saucers, wondering what had just happened.

I did notice that in future walks, the dogs checked the air very carefully when they left the house to make sure that the moose calf wasn't nearby. During our walks past that location years later, Brill always glanced furtively in the direction from which the calf had launched his attack.

Within a month, Brownie had finally blossomed into a healthy, strong little ungulate. I had switched him onto a commercial cow calf milk substitute, which he had taken to readily, once his stomach and digestion had settled. He was also eating more and more organic material in the form of dead leaves, and decaying sedges from the shore of the pond. I presumed this was the calves' version of Pablum. At times, his eating habits made me gag. The decaying vegetation he pulled from the bottom of the pond had a strong, fetid smell that didn't seem to bother him, but was putrid enough to turn my stomach.

He also took a liking to predigested aspen leaves … in the form of forest tent caterpillars! Super abundant that summer, the caterpillars, in their migration from one side of the beaver pond to the other, would often climb up what they sensed was an aspen tree, not realizing that it was only a stump left behind by the beavers. When the caterpillars got to the top of the gnawed-off stump, a foot or so off the ground, they would sway confusedly, looking for the tree's top. Their motion would catch the eye of the ever-vigilant calf. They, too, were treated as intruders to his pond, so he flailed at them with his hooves. I had been observing this from the distance, but didn't understand why he stopped his attack, sniffed the messy mass and then start to lick the stump. Finally, I went to investigate and soon wished I hadn't. The disgusting, shiny, green-and-fuzzy-blue remains must have had some initial appeal for him to take the first taste. After that, he was hooked! I can't say how often he savoured this boreal gourmet delight, because seeing it once was enough—I coveted my breakfast too much to view this event deliberately again. His preoccupation with the congregating masses of squirmy little caterpillars made me avert my eyes on more than one occasion.

I'm not sure how much of his eating behaviour was normal. I don't know if his mom would have signalled to him that this was not normal forage. During my years of rehabilitating wildlife, I have noticed that even wild youngsters, like young human children, go through an exploratory stage when everything goes into the mouth.

There is a local misconception that no bird or beast will eat tent caterpillars. Presumably they, like many other brightly coloured caterpillars, have compounds that make them taste bitter—maybe they are even slightly toxic. Still, some creatures have adapted to eating them, at least in small amounts. I have observed insectivorous birds such as chickadees and warblers picking up the smaller caterpillar stages and feeding them to their young, after first wiping off the coloured hairs on a branch. I have even had reports from folks who said they had seen black bears high in the branches of big aspen feasting on the hordes of tent caterpillars. It's common practice for bears in early spring to feed on the tiny, tender new leaves of aspen, often climbing high into the canopy and out onto small branches to reach them. Once the leaves reach full growth, though, the bears no longer find them palatable. But something encourages bears back into the treetops during caterpillar invasions. Maybe these omnivores realize, as the moose calf did, that mature aspen leaves taste okay if something else has eaten them first.

By midsummer, the calf seemed to be totally at ease around the beaver pond, and spent much time exploring the shallow waters and sedge-lined shores by himself or walking with me. In our evening exercise sessions, he seemed to respond to that stillness that forms in the woods at eventide. He would walk silently through the soft mud, sniffing and testing the air, occasionally making a soft contact call, which I would answer in like manner. Surprisingly, the call that the calf made was not all that different from the soft calls that emanated from inside the beaver lodge at the edge of the pond. I'm not sure if they were communicating at some level or not, or if the similarity was limited only to my human ears, but they certainly sounded very much alike. As the evening set in, the beavers would emerge cautiously, testing the air for predators, before starting another hard night's work.

An incident that I can see clearly in my mind to this day occurred as I watched Brownie standing at the water's edge, facing the pond. His head was lowered, his ears perked as far forward as possible and his brown eyes were as wide open as they could be. Floating in the water, facing him, was Eh, the beaver, with his broad tail curled and cocked in preparation to slap or spring. Pound for pound, they were close to the same weight. Their noses were only a couple of feet apart: Brownie's soft, dewy eyes bulging in excitement, the beaver's beady, black eyes glittering back at him. I remembered the wood frogs, the dogs and even my own personal episode with the stubborn bull calf when he was angry. I also remembered Eh's never-ending efforts to drive all ducks and dogs from his domain.

This could be a very interesting confrontation, I thought. It certainly was a beautiful scene. As they squared off, I watched their reflections in the calm waters of the pond, the setting sun gilding their backs with soft highlights.

A loud explosion broke my reverie. Mud, dirty water, and moose calf flew in different directions. The beaver, ready to go about his evening task, had tired first of the standoff and had brought his massive tail down hard on the water. By the time I cleaned the pond goop from my glasses, I could just make out the back end of the calf, disappearing across the field. After convincing him to come out of the dense bush where he was hiding, I led a rather subdued bully into the compound that night, nervously glancing over his shoulder when the occasional beaver tail slapped across the pond.

It seemed for a while after Brownie's unnerving encounter with Eh that he preferred daytime ventures to the pond. He would race from one shore to the other, occasionally stumbling, head and snout first, into the beaver canals carved into the clay bottom. His appearance was often humorous: with his gangly legs springing out from side to side as he ran, teeth bared, ears pressed back and pond water spraying all over, he resembled the cartoon character Yosemite Sam wildly riding his bony old army mule. That army mule's gallop would aptly describe the calf's gait when he ran. I could almost hear the "Heyahh, mule, heyahh, HEYAHH!" of ol' Yosemite as the calf approached. I only wished that the "Whoa, mule, whoa, WHOA!" which normally followed would have worked on the calf, because as I watched him run, he would turn to me and bear down on my location at the pond's edge. If I didn't stand beside a small tree, or carry my walking stick, the sound of his dainty little hoof connecting with my kneecap would ring throughout the valley.

As ever-increasing numbers of feathered patients arrived at the rehab centre, heralding the fledgling season for birds, Christy, also a wildlife custodian, would give me a breather from time to time with the time-consuming "bear watch." She would keep watch and walk with the calf as it patrolled the beaten moose trails at the edge of the field, and both would battle with the swarm of mosquitoes. She also knew not to talk human talk, or pat or handle the calf. She, too, would wear dark brown clothing, something that I hoped would form a familiar image for the calf. I know that there is a view that most animals, particularly crepuscular ones, do not see colour well. In *Ecology and Management of North American Moose*, Tony Bubenik refers to research (Johnson 1901, Witzel, et al. 1978, Weiss 1981) on the presence of both rods and cones in the eyes of moose, with the conclusion that the cones allow the moose to see colours. I have noticed that they will respond to things that are different colours, and used a red pail for his treats. If I wanted to lead him anywhere he was reluctant to go, I took the red pail with me and he followed willingly. So if nothing else, there are visible differences in the shades they see, or auras that emit from at least some hues or colours. Brown was a good colour to select as it represented the non-threatening colour of another calf and since I knew that moose hunters, if they valued their lives and obeyed regulations, would not wear brown while hunting. There was still a problem with him recognizing and not being afraid of the human image though, and I wasn't sure how to break him of that habituation.

Contact with other humans, for the most part, was very restricted. I was forced to turn away friends who arrived unannounced with their children, intent on helping me to feed and play with the calf. I had to explain to them that this little animal's only hope at life was to be afraid of humans. The dubious looks from the adults would usually end when I showed them the masses of bruises on my legs and knees, results of the calf's version of "play." The sight of my mangled legs convinced the parents that maybe he wasn't the vision of cuteness they held in their mind. The kids, psyched up by the parents during the ride out about this wonderful little animal they were told they would be meeting, weren't so easily convinced. I know the kids were very disappointed. I felt like a heel when one little fellow sobbed, "You're a mean lady," but I had to do what was best for the calf. And whether the children knew it or not, I was also protecting them from carrying away vivid bruises like the ones adorning my legs.

By the end of July, the calf was consuming ten litres of calf milk replacer a day, plus natural browse and commercial deer food. He had such incredible suction when he fed, he could collapse the side of the two-litre plastic pop bottle with its attached lamb's nipple, in one long draw. Maybe this explains the long, drawn look on the faces of the moose cows I have seen. Having to feed just one calf would be draining to say the least, but some cows have twins or even triplets. Maybe this even explains why some of the poor frazzled cows just walk out to the middle of a busy highway and stand there, too!

Despite his desire to continue to drink most of his meals, this calf was ready to be weaned and, more importantly, he was at the stage of development where his future needed to be determined. I reasoned that at my property, he would have had the space and habitat to free range, and since there are often moose in the area, he would also possibly have a chance to mix with his own kind. But my rehabilitation centre was not equipped with the required minimal facilities to continue his care into the fall and winter. Even though my closest neighbours are a few kilometres away and we own more than 150 acres, I did not have protective fencing in place, and I did not have the man-power or means to keep him for a full year. In addition, my licensing and facilities were not suited for his later stages of development, so raising him to release in this area was not possible.

The Ontario Ministry of Natural Resources Wildlife in Captivity manager provided me with the information I needed. I telephoned one of the recommended licensed facilities, 'Solitudes,' and decided early in my conversation with the custodians there that this indeed would be the perfect spot for him.

Their typical wards were white-tailed deer, which often carry a parasite, *P. tenuis*, or a brain worm, which is often fatal if passed on to moose. Therefore, he would have to be kept in a compound where deer were excluded. But the good folks at Solitudes, in Eastern Ontario, were ready to start building his new home. My job was to figure out how to get the now not-so-little guy from one side of Ontario to another.

The regional commuter plane service that had brought Brownie's milk to me was my next contact. Once again, Bearskin Airways came to my rescue. After several calls back and forth, arrangements made and arrangements can-

celled, there finally came a day when they had the right carrier with a suitable
cargo hold stationed in Kenora. Encouraged that there were no last-minute
cancellations, I hurriedly rounded up a few friends to help me get Brownie
into the carrier. I sought out folks who had calm, quiet voices who wouldn't
seem threatening to the calf. That morning before leaving for work, I had
been able to persuade Brownie to enter the room that I had set up in the old
house for him to use on stormy days. It had been several weeks since he had
been inside there, so I wasn't sure what his temperament would be like when
I returned home to ready him for his trip.

We backed my Ford half-ton up to the door and after putting the tailgate
down for easier loading, I entered the building first with my crew in tow. As I
entered, I made a soft contact call to let the calf know I was with this group of
strange people. Brownie was nervous and jumpy, having never seen so many
humans at once. I had left the large dog carrier (Great Dane-sized!) that he
was to be shipped in where he could see and smell it for several days, hoping
he would no longer find it scary. I would regularly toss his favourite treats
into the kennel and he was used to entering it to feed on his goodies. When
it came down to luring him into the carrier for real with the treats I tossed in,
I wasn't so lucky. He sensed my anxiety and balked at the carrier. It looked as
if I now had no option but to wrestle him into the carrier. I figured I had one
chance if I could take him by surprise. If I failed the first time, he would likely
kick the bejesus out of me.

"Here goes nothing, folks—we have to try to hold him and fold him into
the kennel," I instructed my loading crew. Picturing this scenario, my friends
couldn't help but grin. While I psyched myself up for this action, some come-
dian in our midst started humming the Kenny Rogers tune "The Gambler."
Brownie let me approach him, and when I felt the time was right, I wrapped
my arms around his legs and lifted, straining under his weight, while Joan
gently guided his long neck and head into the carrier. Thankfully, the rest of
the body just followed. The strange popping noises in my back and neck assured me that a visit to my chiropractor would be in order when this was all
over. All in all, once all four of his feet were off the ground, it was surprisingly
easy to get Brownie into the kennel carrier, and we found that as long as we
kept the kennel in motion, he would lie down. This was a safer position for
him to be in with less chance of him damaging his legs or hooves. Off to the
airport we raced, so the moose could fly the "Bear."

I had mixed emotions as I sat with him, waiting for the rest of the cargo to be loaded on to the plane. Mostly though, I felt sad as I listened to his soft, short calls, and I was concerned that he might panic in flight. Each strange sound made his ears flash and twitch, as he peered nervously out of the small openings in the carrier. I had fastened a solid piece of cardboard over the metal meshed door, as there was the chance if he did panic, he would flail at the door, damaging his hooves or dewclaws. The cardboard would help to prevent this from happening and also too many well-wishers from peering in, possibly frightening him even more.

When I left him at the tarmac for the airline staff to load him onto Bearskin's turbo prop Metro, Brownie started his long, piteous contact calls. I felt badly at the time that the poor crew and passengers were to be subjected to this caterwauling. I was to learn later from the staff that once the plane started moving and there was vibration and motion, he calmed down, uttering only the occasional forlorn bellow.

On the receiving end, Christine and Pete at Solitudes were equally apprehensive as to the calf's welfare during and after the flight. Once he was unloaded from the cargo hold, they knew they had to get him out of the carrier and transfer him into the special trailer they use for transporting their wards. Amazingly, he was reasonably calm and sedate after his adventure. Moreover, when he saw the bottle of formula waiting for him, it was all he focused on. Using the bottle for enticement, they were able to steer him into the trailer.

I was told the road trip to his new home was also relatively uneventful. When Christine and Peter delivered him to his new habitat, a reinforced enclosure originally built for whitetail fawns, he took it all in stride. He seemed to be on his best behaviour and settling in well.

Back in Kenora, with the black and blue souvenirs on my knees faded, and my shins showing only a slight greenish tinge, I started to feel guilty. I started thinking of what I had done to these poor, trusting people. They had been so willing to help out, and I had taken advantage of their kindness. I risked a phone call ... just to check on how things were going.

Christine answered. "Oh, hi Lil!"

A good sign! Christine was still talking to me. Things can't be going all that badly, I thought.

"Yes, Bruce—that's what we call him—is getting along very well. We have him in a secluded enclosure where we can keep an eye on him, but where he can't see us. That way we can limit his exposure to humans," Christine explained.

Another good sign … they even renamed him, so he can't be too unpopular, I thought to myself.

I had called him "Brownie," as that was what Andy's boys had named him. But Brownie no longer suited this sturdy young animal. Bruce was a good strong name, and I was sure my Bruce wouldn't be taken aback to have this spirited calf as a namesake.

Christine then went on to describe how the calf had found a substitute for my kneecaps. An apple tree sapling, which stood in the centre of his new enclosure, caught his attention early in his stay. First, it was merely the recipient of the perfunctory sideways kick as he raced, bucking and snorting, from one end of the enclosure to the other. When he tired of this unresponsive living form, he turned on it, flattened his ears, and according to Christine, "pounded the life out of it." That made me even more grateful that he was now in their capable hands. I recalled the gardening incident, and considered his ever-increasing body mass, and knew he could have now done me serious damage, even unintentionally.

"He found another form of exercise, too," Christine said.

She went on to describe how he spent a portion of each day running up and down the hillside sounding like a shaggy locomotive, legs pumping and chest heaving. This was good for him, as it was all necessary exercise and preparation for the strength and dexterity he would require once released to the wild.

Christine and Peter had in the past proved themselves to be experts in handling the prim, porcelain-like whitetail fawns, but they now had their hands full with the "bull calf in the china shop." He ruled supreme in his enclosure, even putting the run on the mild-mannered chipmunks that dared venture to the feeding dish to steal treats. I guess I could grant the calf that indiscretion, as even Beeper the buck fawn I had raised a few years prior would try to mash these little striped thieves as they ran off with his grapes.

The young of all species experience boredom if they aren't challenged enough. While exercise is very important, growing minds must also be regularly stimulated to become acute and honed for adult life. Rehabilitators have to use their imagination to think of suitable things that a young animal may play with. Whenever possible, the young are provided natural toys: squirrels get hard-shelled nuts; young predators clumps of hide, fur, and feathers; and it's sticks, skulls, and bones for eagles, hawks, and owls. But it seemed that Bruce would make his own fun with whatever was at hand (or, in his case, hoof). His water bucket, for example, provided endless moments of play. He would stick his snout into it and blow air bubbles. When he tired of that, he picked up the bucket in his teeth, spilled out its content, and after dropping it, gave it a parting kick, just for good measure. Massive animals like moose can use their cloven extremities to pound and pulverize a predator, imaginary or otherwise, into the ground. Yet when their nose itches, they can take that same mighty hoof and gently scratch the silky soft skin on the inside of their nostrils, or that tiny leathery patch called the rhinarium above their top lip.

Friends of Christine and Pete who help out around Solitudes figured they knew of a toy he couldn't destroy. They added a Jolly Ball to his enclosure. These heavy rubber balls are made for the amusement of horses, tigers, bears, and other captive animals. Predictably, they figured it would hold up to Bruce's attention, too.

Perhaps its fat, round shape resembled Eh the beaver too much, because after some escalating hard play, it too was trampled to death. I'm sure he was having flashbacks of that evening's scary encounter with Eh as he stomped the ball into the ground. To me it seemed there could be no other reason for such pent-up aggression.

Because of his increasing size and possible encounters with humans in his new location, Bruce could not range free as he did on our property. That made cutting and delivering his favourite browse to him in huge quantities an everyday necessity. His favourite foods were striped maple, hobblebush and balsam fir. This buffet was supplemented with calf manna, a commercial pellet food.

According to Christine, it didn't take long for his digestive system to become strong and forgiving. He started eating almost everything without repercussions, including, when he sucked too vigorously, the accidental ingestion of rubber nipples from his bottles of formula. As he continued to grow, his supplement was changed to Moose Breeder pellets, up to ten or twelve pounds of it a day.

Bruce grew and grew under the watchful eyes of the Solitudes crew.

# Outfoxed!

Although my life was quieter without the moose calf to tend to, I was still kept very busy tending to less demanding but ever-increasing numbers of wild patients. Every once in a while, though, I still expected to see a gangly, long-legged brown missile launching itself down the trail or standing in the pond, reflecting. The dogs seemed to miss the excitement of having this big and neat-smelling animal around. Although they knew chasing the calf was forbidden, they could still pretend to track it through the woods when we went for walks. To be sure, I had almost complete trust in Heidi's nose. I had learned that even with the windows closed, Heidi was able to smell animals, including bears, from inside the house. Still, early one morning, I just didn't believe her when she sounded her low growl, then stood on her hind legs, staring out the window into the early morning sun. She generally reserved this posture for the moose calf, but the moose was thousands of miles away.

When the low but not too worried growl from our old dog gave me warning that there was something foreign but not too formidable lurking outside, I left the comfort of my bed, went to the window, and opened it. The dew was just starting to burn off, and the fresh, clean scent of the early morning air filled the room. Heidi stood beside me at the open window, testing the air, growling softly, and indicating something was around, but her actions also told me there was no real danger.

Then, from up the hill, the chickens in their coop started that distinctive distress call known to all poultry farmers as "My gosh, muh … muh … my gosh! Muh … muh … my gosh!" The chickens, too, had seen something amiss. Indeed, an intruder was near.

As a movement caught my attention I looked down to the large boulders piled along the edge of the septic field. I could see a familiar friend, an old chipmunk, stretched out and warming himself in the morning sun. One of his back legs, stiff and shriveled, identified him from the other chipmunks that called this big rock pile their home. Three years ago, this guy had been in my wildlife rehab centre, the victim of a housecat left outside to hunt. The leg would never again be totally functional, but by receiving food and security while he adapted to a three-legged lifestyle, the chipmunk had reached a grand old age.

I caught another movement out of the corner of my eye and then in a flash of red, a fox pounced. Too quick for me to call a warning, the fox was on top of the boulder snapping at the chipmunk. The chipmunk, by no means pusillanimous in the face of death, lunged in a final brave defiance right into the jaws of the fox. Their battle was over in an instant and there was nothing I could do. I felt terrible. The chipmunk had shown me that even with his disabilities, he could lead a happy, productive life. Despite his traumatic experiences with me during the resetting of his leg, followed by confinement while he healed, he seemed to have forgiven me and forgotten his time of trauma. Once released on our property, he never hesitated to run up to greet me and grab my offering of food. And now he was dead. I know it was nature taking its course, but that didn't make me feel any better.

I glared angrily at the fox, but he was too busy with his prize to even look up. He was a big male, busily collecting food for his vixen-in-waiting and their developing pups. He would likely cache this tasty morsel of chipmunk as he sought out more food, coming back for it at a later time. Sure enough, I watched as he poked the lifeless little body under a tuft of grass, spreading the blades over it with his nose to hide his prize from prying eyes.

As he started to leave, he glanced up and snarled. I followed his gaze and saw a raven watching from a nearby tree. He whirled back to the chipmunk and picked it up again, glancing at the raven with what appeared to be annoyance. For a long time, they glared at each other, and then it seemed the fox had won the staring contest, as the raven croaked and flew away. When the raven was out of sight, the fox once again stuck his treasure under some dried sedges, carefully arranging the dead grass to conceal the body. Satisfied, he trotted off.

I heard a chortle from above, and saw the raven perched high on my rooftop. It, too, had seen the actions of the fox from his lookout point. He had feigned a departure until the fox had moved on. Then the raven flew to the ground and started to systematically poke and pull at tuffs of grass along the visible trail the fox had made walking through the dew-covered vegetation. His black head bobbed, as he sauntered and poked in the weeds. His motions reminded me of a scene in a British movie, with the London bobbies poking their nightsticks in the bushes of some park, searching for clues or a hidden body. Like the bobbies, the raven knew a prize was hidden somewhere in the tangled weeds. With persistence, he would find it.

I couldn't leave my little friend's earthly remains to this gory fate, even if it was a natural turn of events. I rationalized my sentimentality as being scientific curiosity; that I merely wanted to check how well the damaged leg I had set years before had healed. I walked through the lawn grass to where I had seen the fox hiding away the chipmunk. The raven flew up as I approached and settled on a branch nearby. It took me a few minutes to find the well-camouflaged little body, which was stashed under some tall, dead sedge beside the lawn. I gently picked up his still warm body and stroked it.

The raven, which had been watching me, suspected something was up and soared over to land on the ground nearby, peering through the sedges at me. He *gronked* his objections, but overall seemed to accept the loss of his stolen prize rather well. Who knows? Maybe he thought there were more bodies hidden out there. I ignored the raven's mutterings and carried the dead little chipmunk back to the house, stroking him as I walked. Later I buried him in my version of Potter's Field. No recycling for this little hero; he had earned a proper interment.

When I reached the balcony of the house, I stopped to watch for a few moments to see how the events in the field would unfold now. I caught a glimpse of the fox heading back to the spot in the field where I had gathered up my little friend. Finding his prize gone, the fox turned his anger on the raven, who had given up his search and was now perched on a sedge-covered hummock. They both snapped and hopped at each other, before each gave up in disgust. I wonder if the fox received a similar confrontation from his vixen when he returned to their den, empty-mouthed.

I guessed that in the fox's world, as in ours, if it seems too good to be true, it probably is. Easy meals just aren't meant to be. Later in the year, I was able to catch a glimpse of his vixen with her half-grown kits. I watched as they threaded their way single file down to the shore of our little lake for a drink of fresh water.

When I saw the grey, fuzzy fox kits, hopping and playing in the filtered forest light waiting for their hard-working dad to bring them food, I found myself feeling slightly less upset about the loss of the chipmunk. It also reminded me of another sweet little bundle that was delivered to me many years ago.

The little kit vixen was found on a cottage lawn on Lake of the Woods, wandering on its own. The folks who first encountered it tried to find the rest of the litter, or its mom, or even its den, to no avail. By the time they had exhausted all the possibilities, the little fox had been too long without food to survive without some intervention. They phoned to ask my advice, but I was hesitant to accept the kit. While rabies occurrences are extremely low in our part of northwestern Ontario, I would still have had to treat it as if it were rabid, until I could be sure there was no risk. I found out after taking the first of a series of shots that make up the rabies vaccine, I reacted badly to something in the inoculate mixture, so I had to be cautious.

However, when the call came in from the lake, I believed that if I maintained a common-sense hygiene regime, the possibility of spread of any disease or parasites was minimal. Although I agreed to have a look, there was some reluctance on my part.

I think it was the beautiful grey eyes and lamb-like face that helped me make up my mind to say yes, that I would care for the little fox. A story by Ernest Thompson Seton I had read as a child came to mind when I looked into that sweet face. In *The Springfield Fox* the injustices of mankind towards animals are described. At one point, a vixen takes drastic measures to free her captive kit from the hand of human captors, feeding her chained and collared kit poisoned chicken heads left by the farmer to kill her. That sad story of how the little fox died left me with a feeling of guilt and responsibility as a child, and a mission to redeem human nature when the opportunity offered itself. Here, perhaps, would be my chance.

Unlike the fox in Seton's story, this one was not restrained with collar and chain. Instead, it had a warm, fur-lined bed in a dark, den-like box. Stuffed toys similar to her in size and colour kept her silent company. A hot water bottle and a mirror provided additional psychological and physical comfort. A shallow pan with sand provided her litter box. In their natural den, she would have a separate area for her toilet, so the young fox took naturally to using a litter box. Foxes seem to be more catlike than dog-like in much of their behaviour, and pups will scratch and cover their scat if it's near the den, just as cats do. If hunting or travelling away from the den, though, they don't seem so concerned with covering their spoor. Some actually seem to proudly display it on smooth rocks and high points along a trail. I remember pulling over one time to pick up an expensive snowmobile mitt that had apparently fallen from a passing vehicle onto the roadway. My intent was to hang it on a branch in sight of the road for the owner to reclaim it should he or she pass that way again. I picked it up but quickly dropped it, as the scent of fox musk wafted into my nose. When I drove the same route later that week, I saw the fox carrying the mitt in his mouth along the ditch. In case he decided to dash onto the road, I slowed down to avoid hitting it. As I slowed, I watched the fox trot to a flat open spot in the ditch line and drop the mitt. After a show of arranging and circling the sodden mitt, he added a fresh spray of scent before trotting off. He had his own mobile scent post. Remembering that strong, tomcat-like scent on the mitt made me glad that my little ward was a vixen.

I wouldn't have to put up with the strong smell that dog foxes produce and spread around with gay abandon.

For the first few days, feeding the kit was a challenge. It was difficult convincing her to eat anything I offered. I tempted her with several types of food, from liquids to mush to solids. Judging by her stage of development and dentine structure, I assumed mom wouldn't have let her nurse too much longer, and would be weaning her other kits already. The vixen had likely been chewing food into mush for her kits so I tried to match the consistency of the fare she may have been providing her young. My initial offerings of mashed mouse, ground grouse, riced rat, and chopped chickens were left untouched. She didn't trust me. And I'm sure she missed her family. Her only source of nutrition for the first few days she was with me was commercial orphan puppy formula. But I knew the formula did not provide enough nutrition for a growing kit.

Then, by accident, I bumped the mirror I had placed in her little den as I was setting down the food. In her baby eyes, she must have thought one of her siblings was getting the jump on the shapeless blob of flesh I had put in the dish. She raced to the food, covering it with her little body, ears back, tail thrashing, lips curled, all the while making strange coughing sounds. As she bolted down the food, she continued to snarl and mutter ferociously at the image in the mirror. After, as long as the mirror was close to her dish, feeding was no longer a problem. Once I deposited the food into her dish and was out of her sight, she would wolf it down, glaring and coughing at her image as she did.

Her makeshift den took up one whole corner of our new garage. Since we hadn't even christened the new structure with the vehicles it was built for, there were no oils or antifreeze spills to worry about. She could have the free run of the garage without getting into anything dangerous, even though she spent most of her time around her bedding area. She was wary and as soon as she heard a noise, she would zip back to her "den." When I looked inside, only a small, black, moist nose would be visible, twitching in the air of her doorway, scenting to determine who the intruder was.

She grew quickly, and seemed intelligent and quick to learn.

I knew she would need more and more independence and freedom, if she were to develop into a normal fox. When I figured that the time was right, I left the garage door open a crack one day and let her make up her own mind whether she wanted to explore the big world. As a precaution, I set up baby monitors near the garage door to warn me of marauding neighbour dogs, or if she were in distress. I had a few more chores to finish before I went in for the evening and I set about doing them, while keeping an eye on the partially opened door. While I tended to my outside work, I caught a glimpse of a little black nose appearing out of the gloom of the doorway. Soon, a face followed the nose. With eyes closed in bliss, she sniffed the wondrous smells on the wind and took in a whole new world. Then out she stepped, and if her expression could have been translated, I'm sure it would have been something like, "wow!"

I continued with my chores, keeping an eye on her as she explored. I wondered if she would bolt for freedom, never to return, or if she would treat the garage like her den site—a place of safety. She walked, sniffed, and peed, walked, sniffed, and peed, effectively blazing a trail for her speedy return home, if a run was necessary. It was soon apparent that she did not want to run away, but rather wanted to continue exploring at her own speed. Her body language, which included tensing up at any strange sound, indicated she was nervous and ready to rip back into the safety of the garage in a twinkle. I wasn't sure how to call an end to her first evening of adventure, but I knew I had to go in for the night. I didn't want to leave her out in case she encountered dogs or ran out to the highway. My problem solved itself as a low-flying raven *gronked* a greeting as it passed over my yard, alarming the little fox. Quick as a flash, the fox disappeared into the darkness of the garage. I quietly closed the garage door and retired for the evening, pleased with the milestone the fox had reached.

One of my routine evening chores was to clean out one of the hawk pens near the back of our property. This unsavoury task included raking up fecal matter and debris, and removing leftover chicken, grouse, and squirrel bones from the hawks' past meals. A very unpleasant task, but necessary nonetheless.

I was too intent on my chore to realize the pan I was filling with the hawks' castoff meals was just as swiftly emptying. I caught a furtive movement out of the corner of my eye, and in the evening gloom saw the little fox disappearing into the garage with something in her mouth. When I went to check on her, I was met with coughs, snarls, and tail-thrashing, though I knew they were only bluffs. Sure enough, her little food cache, or midden, which was right by her bed, had grown considerably. A pile of kibble and dog biscuits was covered over with the furred and feathered remnants of the hawks' meals I had been gathering from the flight cage.

While the kit was preoccupied with her evening meal, I removed the sharper bones that had the potential to injure her. Then I left her to enjoy the plethora of smells and sensations emitting from her scavenged horde. As I walked out of the garage, I turned to see her with feet in the air, eyes blissfully closed, lips pulled over her teeth in a grin, wiggling around to rub the rancid smells into her fur, just as I'm sure my dog would have done had she found these odorous goodies.

The kit spent many evenings exploring the backyard under my watchful eye. The garden was of particular interest, and cutworms, grubs, and carpenter ants first became her play toys, then a snack when their wiggles wore out or their packaging burst. Large grasshoppers provided great amusement to her, and to me, as she hopped after them, pouncing, then searching under her paws for the victim. Often, while she searched her pounce zone, she seemed unable to comprehend that she might have missed her victim, the fortunate invertebrate having crawled into the tall grass. From time to time, I would harden my heart and release a domestic mouse from my breeding supply for her to hunt. Her hunting ability became keen under this live training. Once she perfected the hang of mousing, not only did the number of escapee white mice dwindle, but the wild mouse population in my shed was put in check, too.

She seemed particularly proud of her four-footed attack. From a tense, standing stop, she would leap into the air and bring her feet together in a perfect four-point pounce. The object of her attention would be tossed and flipped, and then tossed some more. When she tired of the game she would give it one final flip in the air, and into her mouth it would disappear. My initial concerns that she would have no mother to teach her standard hunting techniques proved unfounded.

Best of all, as her foster mom, I did not have to try to teach her Fox Pouncing 101. I'm sure my neighbours would have reported me to the proper authorities had they seen me bouncing through the yard on all fours.

My reputation in the neighbourhood had been marred enough from a previous incident early one morning when I had been returning from collecting fresh browse for one of my wards, when I spotted a freshly killed squirrel on the highway.

Great! I thought, hawk food!

I was dressed in baggy, khaki clothes. I likely had bed-head, and I know I was still half-asleep. Somewhat groggily, I quickly checked both ways and, confident no one was watching and no traffic was coming, I scurried across to the centre line and pounced upon my prize. After I dropped it into the baggy pockets of my coat, I glanced up to see my new neighbours pulling out of their driveway. They were staring through the windshield of their car, their jaws hanging in disbelief. I believe she was mouthing the words, "Did you see that?" to her husband. I grinned sheepishly, waved, and scurried off the highway back into the ditch. I half-expected to see a care package and canned goods on my doorstep that night, but instead the new neighbours just kept a safe distance from me, looking askance if I made eye contact with them.

Sometimes, the little fox preferred a more vegan diet. There was an extremely good blueberry crop that year and whenever I had some spare time I would walk from the house to nearby patches to pick. She must have decided to follow my scent trail and discovered the patches for herself. After gorging in the berry patch all night, she would come home and, before retiring in the garage for the day, invariably leave a purple memory of her meal on my doorstep.

These ventures away from home seemed to give her a new sense of independence. Her return visits became less frequent, and eventually she only came home if the weather was cool, or if it had been stormy for a few days. These extended sojourns proved to me her hunting skills were developing satisfactorily. But since I felt she still needed a backup food source, I would subtly leave a meal, in the form of a road-killed squirrel or chipmunk, at the treed edge of our lot for her to find. The food would disappear overnight, and I assumed she was the one taking it, not another fox or a skunk.

When she was in my direct care, I tried hard to ensure the kit and our dog avoided contact. This, I hoped, would make her wary of all dogs, and not think that they were potential friends. She was mesmerized by Heidi's scent, though, and would check the dog's favourite areas with a thorough sniffing. But now that she was coming and going on her own time, I couldn't always make sure Heidi was in the house when the fox returned. As it turned out, I didn't have to worry about Heidi hurting the kit, as it seemed my dog was leery of this odd dog that had lived in our garage. If the fox happened to come home when Heidi was tied out on her long leash, she would frantically bark to come back into the house. I would look out in time to see poor Heidi pressed to the door, with the young fox in the "down in front," universal canine come-play-with-me body language. Heidi was having none of that strange little dog, not if she could help it. But the fox loved to torment her. I once caught her tugging at Heidi's tie-out leash trying to pull her back into the yard. Sometimes I would catch her running away with Heidi's food dish.

It is no wonder Heidi maintained a grudge towards all foxes after all that.

One of the last visits I had with the little vixen took place in late fall as I was preparing my garden for winter. I had just dumped a big pile of leaves in the centre of the garden for mulching when suddenly, the pile exploded in a blur of red. The little vixen had flung herself on top of the leaf litter, and was now facing me, coughing and tail thrashing in what I now recognized as a fox greeting, and with a big canine smile we attribute to dogs. She treated me to a wonderful greeting, nipping and rubbing against my legs, catlike. I couldn't resist offering her a handout. I knew I shouldn't reinforce her familiarity with human food, but I thought a freshly thawed piece of venison would be okay. I felt better when she picked through my offering with disdain. Obviously she wasn't starving, and hopefully she preferred the fare she must now be catching on her own. She trotted around the yard sniffing, and then disappeared into the open garage. When I peeked inside, I saw her sniffing around her old "den." I still hadn't removed her bedding, perhaps subconsciously hoping she would return, but mostly the cleanup had lagged because I had been so busy with other orphans. Without so much as a "Thanks, and be seeing ya" she took off out the garage door and into the woods, carrying her surrogate littermate, a stuffed toy she had once cuddled for comfort.

Bruce and I found that toy a year or so later, sodden and torn, at the edge of a well-used fox den in the gravel pits behind our house. By all evidence, she had survived the year, and by the looks of the tiny little footprints in the sand around the den's entrance, had raised her own family of kits.

The only other clue of her continued existence came in the form of a telephone call I received the next fall. A lady living some miles down the road from me questioned the antics of a fox in her yard. It seemed it kept playing tug-of-war with her dog's leash, much to her dog's distress. Seems that old habits die hard. I assured her that it was not likely a case of rabies, more likely a fox a little too familiar with humans and domestic dogs.

Since raising and releasing her, we have moved to our present acreage, so I don't know if she ever visited the site of her old stomping grounds again. The foxes out on our new property are, wisely, much more wary of humans. Several folks in the neighbourhood, including me, raise domestic chickens and ducks, which foxes seem to have a weakness for. When I see one now, to save its life, I hoot and holler and chase after it to let it know we don't welcome it at all. Sometimes the dogs join in with shrill barks of displeasure at the intruder.

# Moose on the Loose!

Wildlife rehabilitators, or wildlife custodians, as we are now called in Ontario, often do not have the opportunity to monitor the lives of their wards once they have been released to the wild. Sometimes that may be just as well, as even youngsters raised by their natural mothers often do not survive the first year of their lives or, for that matter, the first few months. I had been fortunate with Eh and the kit fox in that I was able to observe them as they matured. This makes the argument "why even bother," at least from my personal perspective, far more defensible. Even the disabled little chipmunk had been around for a long period of time, considering the numbers of predators always out there, looking for food.

I kept thinking about the moose calf and how he was doing. I phoned Solitudes, eager for information on his latest shenanigans. I knew that soon Christine and Pete would be making the arrangements to release him back into the wild. Because he was a yearling, it would be no easy feat to load and transport him to his new home.

In the wild, calf moose stay with their mother for at least one full year, and some may even hang around with the cow until reaching maturity at about three years of age. This is especially true of cow calves. Young bulls, however, can become too unruly and familiar with their mothers, and be driven away from them. It is not uncommon to see groups of bulls travelling together all year round, only showing intolerance or aggression with each other, or to newcomers, during breeding season.

Two moose hunters told me of separate incidents when, after they had shot a bull out of a group, some of the other bulls from the herd tried to get their downed companion to stand up and run. One conservation officer described how the twin of a yearling bull he had shot made several attempts to lift its dead sibling by putting his head under its front legs and lifting, even though it must have been aware of the dangerous human presence. The man had found this very disturbing, as would most people, if they saw animals showing what seem to be acts of compassion for each other.

While Bruce the moose, transplanted and far from home, would not have a family group to fit into, we all were hopeful his sheer size would help him survive any pushing and shoving that would likely occur when he encountered other moose. As he reached his second summer, which made him both a yearling and a teenager, he was ready to leave his foster parents.

Christine and Pete needed time to prepare for the big event. Bruce was already very leery of humans, and was acting more and more like the bull he was. A yearling, he was already digging rut pits and urinating in them, a common communication medium between moose, which usually occurs during the breeding season, but a behaviour he seemed to be practising earlier in life than usual. I remembered my six-month-old buck fawn acting in a similar fashion. When he found the scrapes of the adult bucks in the fall, he began making his own tiny scrapes and urinating in them, while acting very excited. This communication to members of their own kind is another example of just how hardwired animals are to be what they are. While they learn much from the cow and other members of the population they encounter, they also rely a lot on genetic information for survival.

Arrangements had been made by Christine and Pete to deliver Bruce to a predetermined site that looked, at least to the discerning human eye, like perfect moose habitat. It had lakes, marshes, hills, lots of browse, and dense forest. Best of all, the presence of other moose suggested the area had all the habitat he would need to survive.

However, moving a 650-pound moose is a lot harder than moving a sixty-to seventy-pound calf. He now sported a set of developing antlers. While the antlers were still tender, soft, and easily damaged in their velvet stage, they were surprisingly large for a yearling. Bruce the moose would have to be chemically immobilized and hauled into a stock trailer to be moved safely. And there are so many things that can go wrong when using immobilization drugs on large ungulates. They can suffocate just from lying in one spot, as their massive body weight can press down on their lungs, causing circulation to be cut off to their extremities, resulting in tissue death.

Chemicals can also cause them to regurgitate and drown in their own body fluids. And those are only two of the possible things that could go wrong.

To make sure any medical problems that might arise could be dealt with, Christine and Peter's vet, Dr. Mason, came along to monitor Bruce's vital signs. The vet was also there to make sure the antagonist, a drug used to reverse the effects of the immobilizing drug, was correctly administered. On the sidelines, but providing extra assistance and muscle where needed, were volunteers from the Peterborough Zoo. A YTV television crew, who were on hand to film Bruce's release, were prepared to help if necessary.

After a nail-biting hour-long drive, the caravan reached the release site. Tension grew, as Bruce was slow to react to the reversal drug the vet administered. Finally, after several anxious moments, a dazed and confused young bull moose stood and stretched his long legs, gazing around in bewilderment at the stock trailer, the trucks, vans, and assorted other vehicles. Confronted with the television crew, with their strange faces and smells, he bolted into the bush; his crashing retreat could be heard as he vanished deep into the woods. The moose had entered the world of humans through a camera lens, so it was only fitting he left it behind while being filmed. In the weeks that followed, Pete and Christine made several trips back to the release location to check on Bruce's progress, but found only the occasional moose track and limited evidence of browsing. They never did catch sight of him again. The fact he wasn't hanging around the release site and never barrelled out of the bushes to greet them were good signs he was safe and comfortable in his new environment. With Bruce the moose free and loose, I am sure the folks at Solitudes felt the same weight lifted from their shoulders as I had when I had put the calf on Bearskin Air, and on to the next step in his life. Raising a moose is very demanding on time and resources, and once they had released the calf,

I'm sure there was an empty feeling in their life as there had been in mine for the first while after he left here. More than once, out of habit, I found myself heading down the hill towards his compound to let him out for his evening exercise. The sight of his empty compound reminded me he was gone, and this was no longer my final chore for the evening. Trudging back up the hill, I felt a bittersweet void in my life.

# Fowl Days Ahead

I had come through the winter with only a few patients, most of these the beautiful northern owls that needed overwintering and a steady food source. When the vole and lemming populations in the north are low, owls desperate for food migrate south in large numbers. These stately birds came into my care after either being injured by vehicles, or being picked up by someone who found them lying in the snow, too weak to fly. Once their injuries healed and they could be safely released, I had time to clean pens, and prepare for the next influx of summer babies.

If and when things were quiet on the rehabilitation front, I could relax and enjoy life. On those rather rare occasions, Bruce and I could even get in some fishing and camping. I was not able to enjoy these luxuries when I had Bruce the moose or any of my more demanding little wards to take care of.

Northwestern Ontario has so much to offer in the way of natural pleasures; we never have to travel too far to savour our fleeting moments of freedom. There is something for everyone, whether it is the non-consumptive user or people harvesting from the resources. The lakes and trails entice hikers, cottagers, canoeists, photographers, hunters, trappers, and fishers into all its nooks and crannies, at one time of the year or another. During sojourns similar to the ones Bruce and I take into the backwoods, humans often encounter or surprise the permanent residents of the area. And all too often we also become intruders into breeding, nesting, or nursery habitat. The first baby I was to receive for the season was Janice, the unwilling victim of one such encounter.

A group of fellows out for a day of fishing were plying the waters of a remote and productive shallow river system. Because the river they chose to fish had so little human traffic, it was favoured by many species of waterfowl for nesting and feeding. If I understood the chain of events correctly, this is how the drama unfolded.

The fishermen drifted by an old beaver lodge and were startled as two adult geese took to the air in a rattle of wings. The geese flew off, frantically calling back and forth, obviously distraught. The guys continued fishing until they realized a spectacular event was taking place on the abandoned beaver house. A down-lined nest held goslings, some dried and fluffy, some sticky and wobbly, as well as the remaining clutch of eggs, which were hatching before their eyes. Enthralled by what was happening, they watched from the boat as sticky, matted little goslings spilled out of the nest.

Some of the goslings were strong enough to stand up and focus on their surroundings. It seems after several of the young geese spotted the boat full of fishermen, they jumped into the water and started to swim after it. I can only assume the ones that had just hatched would have been too weak, wobbly, and wet to follow. Perhaps the parents returned to claim these later, or so I can only hope.

As the fellows left their watch and resumed fishing, they trolled down the shore, only to have the goslings follow the shiny aluminum "mom" with its multiple heads. Attempts to shoo the little geese away were met with confusion, a slight hesitation and then a frantic effort to catch up to "mom" again.

There were other interested parties watching this drama unfold. A pair of eagles nesting nearby, reaping the benefits of a river system rich in fish and fowl, were likely thrilled to see the goslings, viewing them as easy, tender food for their hungry chicks. The guys watched in horror as the hapless fluffs, floating unprotected in the open waters, were picked one by one from the water by the eagles. Seeing one last survivor, buzzing around the surface confused and panicked, the fishermen reeled in, swung the boat around and scooped up the little mite.

With their single survivor, the anglers, similar to those who had captured Brownie the moose calf, called off their fishing to make a special trip into the Ministry of Natural Resource's office to try to find me. When I came to the front counter and saw the little gosling standing there, defiantly staring down the amused receptionist, I melted. I forgot how much I was enjoying my reduced workload at home, and Janice came home with me.

Young waterfowl are notorious for the solid imprint they form with the first attentive living (or moving) thing they see when they hatch. Their survival is dependent on them following their mother (or in the case of geese, mother and father). Both the goose and gander will sit by the nest "talking" as the hatching takes place, to ensure they are the first living things their goslings see or hear. In the case of Janice the goose, the intrusion of the humans had broken this moment of bonding, and the consequences for Janice's small family had been severe.

I can recall another example of imprinting, told to me by my husband on his return from a fishing trip. He and his fishing partner were trolling the shores of a lake, searching for the elusive muskellunge. Fan casting a shallow bay, they had seen several large muskies following their lures to the boat, but had not been able to entice any to take the bait. As they moved along the shore, a frantic peeping caught their attention. In the soft, rolling wake of the boat, a small duckling buzzed like a mechanized tub toy, its small feet a blur in its haste to catch up to the motoring vessel.

The young wood duck, likely having hatched out from some nearby high tree cavity, had probably jumped from its downy nest to the forest floor and was working its way towards its mother's calls. Its mother, as is the practice among wood ducks, would have been waiting on the shore of the lake or a nearby pond, trying to keep up a continuous communication with her hatching young. As the brood hatched over the course of a day or two, they would normally work their way, singly, quickly, and—hopefully—undetected, through the camouflaging forest litter to the anxiously waiting mom. Perhaps the approaching boat had caused mom to go silent, and the young duckling, confused, went to the next sound it heard: human voices. Bruce had shooed and splashed at the young fuzzball, but to no avail. He knew not to make any motions or sounds that it might have interpreted as friendly, which would have encouraged it to follow. Tired and perhaps realizing its error, the duckling finally turned and started to buzz the surface back to shore. When Bruce looked back to check its progress, only a large swirl and bubbles marked the waters where the duckling had been, and a long silvery form sunk back into the dark depths.

The powerful effect of imprinting can make raising a single orphaned baby a rehabber's nightmare. The general opinion of waterfowl managers and wildlife custodians is that a single gosling raised by humans can never be successfully released to the wild. I, too, have seen the results of such upbringings and they were invariably sad cases ... tame geese approaching dogs, hunters, kids with sticks, even natural predators such as a fox or a coyote. In many cases, imprinted geese are actually confrontational to any new or strange animal encounter, hissing and jabbing with their necks outstretched. They made for easy prey for mink, dogs, and the like.

But in this case, I decided to cross that bridge when I came to it. First of all, I had to make sure that she (not that I knew for sure it was a she, just her petite manner suggested she might be, as geese are smaller than ganders) had access to the huge quantities of food she needed for her fast-growing body and developing feathers. By the time she reached the size of an adult mallard, she would consume a five-gallon pail of freshly picked grass and clover in a single day. There is a phrase used to describe a hasty event: "like grass through a goose." Geese don't store the foods they eat; instead, their strategy of survival is to process large quantities of highly nutritious foods quickly through their system. I supplemented her huge appetite for grass with mealworms, cutworms, grasshoppers, and grains. I found out by accident that she also loved a kibble-type kitten food, which she ate with gusto, but discovered was not really a suitable food source, and should not have been part of her buffet. I had wrongly assumed that she was getting sufficient calcium, phosphorous, and vitamin D from the other foods I supplied her with and from her time spent outdoors. I would soon find out I had set her up for a dangerous condition called metabolic bone disease, but it wasn't obvious to me in the early stages of her life.

While she was in the downy stage, she had little interest in swimming and would hop out of her bathtub after a few minutes of paddling. (She loved bathing and preening in the fine mist of a spritzer bottle, or under the spray of the lawn sprinkler, though.) A misconception many rescuers have is that foundling waterfowl and baby marine mammals have to be housed in water. To be accommodating, they sometimes keep them floating in a tub of water all day. Youngsters at this tender age, like the gosling I had, just can't thermoregulate their body temperature very well and lose vital body heat quickly. Keeping them wet or in water will often result in hypothermia or pneumonia, both of which usually lead to death.

All young, feathered fledgling birds, not just waterfowl, need to have access to fresh water every day to splash around in and to drink. Bathing helps to encourage them to preen and clean away dirt, feather dust, and down, and to ensure the developing feathers provide the necessary waterproofing birds require. Dirty feathers also have little or no insulating properties and leave the birds susceptible to cold and heat. Preening and cleaning helps to keep the system of hooks and barbules on feathers interlocked properly, effectively creating a physical waterproof barrier. One of my favourite reference books, *Clinical Avian Medicine and Surgery*, states that the primary mechanism which provides waterproofing is this interlocking of feathers, not oil from the uropygial gland, as I once believed. To support this, the authors refer to the fact that some waterfowl do not even have this gland, and in others, if the gland is surgically removed, the birds still retain their waterproofing.

Still, oil from this small gland, located on the bird's back at the base of the tail, does help to condition the feathers. You may have seen a preening bird or duck tweaking this little protrusion with its beak or vigorously rubbing its head on it before working the oil through their feathers. Some research has shown this little gland produces oil when the bird is sunbathing. Somehow the heat irritates the gland, causing it to secrete vitamin D in an oily form. I do know that if I want a captive bird to preen and clean itself, all I have to do is set it into direct sunlight. I have to carefully scrutinize the situation, though, to insure it doesn't overheat in the sun while it grooms.

Placed in the sun, an injured but otherwise healthy bird will start preening and fluffing within minutes. Young birds, healthy or not, which are deprived of sunlight will often have stunted or poorly developed feathers, and they don't seem to develop strong preening instincts. Captive birds that have to be held over the winter should be kept in a room with full-spectrum artificial light so that their feathers remain healthy and they maintain normal molts.

So far, I felt I had been able to provide the gosling with its basic needs: food, water, and sunlight. But what I figured she really needed was companionship. She seemed so lonely! She'd plod along like an old soul, feet flapping like oversized bedroom slippers as she wandered aimlessly, and calling out for company, a void I personally wasn't capable of or willing to fill in my attempt to avoid imprinting.

While our pond was full of waterfowl, excited and loud as they argued over mates and food, none seemed to be ready to accept or even tolerate an orphaned gosling. I tried introducing her to a mated pair of geese, but either they weren't ready for a kid, had a nest of their own, or were part of an extended family from somewhere else. When they saw my gosling, they laid their heads and neck flat on the water, began hissing and honking, and drove the scared little fluffball back to me. After my failed attempts to convince the adult geese to babysit for a while, I gave up and put Janice back into her carrying basket.

I had been so focused on trying to get the gosling adopted that I hadn't realized there was a vital member of the pond missing. The beaver Eh, an icon in my little rehabilitation world, had apparently moved out. He hadn't shown up at the shore, looking for his apple or yam treats, for several days. There had been heavy rains earlier in the spring, and it is during spring rains when young male beavers move from their birth pond and relocate. Perhaps

Eh, responding to his natural instincts, had decided it was time to move on, as things were getting a bit crowded on the pond. He had certainly left behind a legacy. Eh and the female beaver that produced his young had borne at least eleven kits over the years. I would like to think that Eh still lives somewhere downstream from my property. I haven't seen him since he left.

Even though I had been enthralled with Eh and his antics when he was in my care, I was glad when he started living like a beaver in the wild. He had adapted well to life in the pond. Considering he spent his first winter in the basement of our old house, and his second winter alone in a beaver lodge built by inept humans, I think he turned out okay. I had considered my extensive labour, expense, trials, and tribulations while raising him up as a great thing to do once, a neat learning opportunity, but not a task I would take on eagerly a second time.

That is, until a second time came around.

# Oops! I Did it Again!

A call came in from a young lady from the small community of Wabas-eemoong, sixty miles northwest of Kenora. The caller, Shannon, initially telephoned me to get information on the care and feeding of three young beavers her grandfather was tending to. We talked, and upon hearing about the intensive and demanding care these young ones would need to survive, she wondered if maybe I was in a better situation to raise them. The special foods and veterinary care required would be more readily available if the kits were transferred to my rehabilitation centre in Kenora. We discussed possible options for feeding, with yogourts and whipping cream being added to their diet, a poor replacement for mom's rich milk, but given what was available, all we could think of.

A few days after the first call, Shannon and her family decided that I might be in a better position to raise the beavers than they were. We decided on a time and place and the kits were to be brought to me on the caregiver's next trip to Kenora.

Much later, when I talked to the grandfather who had rescued the kits, he told me the story of how he came to take responsibility for these young lives.

As he related the events, his voice couldn't hide how he felt when he realized he had taken the life of an expectant female beaver.

Most experienced and ethical trappers do not relish trapping beavers past the end of March. Fetal beavers are well formed by this time and when the female is pelted or skinned, her advanced stage of pregnancy is only too obvious. It takes a hardened soul not to feel badly.

However, when complaints are voiced by landowners, or road or railroad maintenance crews, regarding property damage from flooding and the loss of trees, trappers may be sent out to remove "nuisance" beavers at any time of the year. If the trapper registered to that particular trapline does not respond, another one will be sent in his place to trap out the nuisance animals. Trappers feel ownership or management obligations to their own line and do not like it when an outsider moves in on their territory. Therefore, they find themselves forced to remove the nuisances, even at times of the year they would normally avoid doing any trapping. Ironically, contracts between governments and companies with the agents assigned for nuisance animal removal often pay more per animal removed than the licensed trapper would receive for a pelt taken during the regulated trapping season.

This particular trapper, acting on a complaint regarding water over a road, had gone in to remove beavers from an adjacent new pond. He saw a large beaver on the shore, near the dammed-up culvert, and shot it. Mother beavers normally stick very close to lodges during the birthing season. Since there was no lodge in sight, the trapper assumed it was a large male, on the move, or the one responsible for creating the new territory. Too late, he realized that high waters had flooded the lodge and it was a female sitting on the remains of the submerged maternity home, soon to give birth. The mother's nice safe lodge had been destroyed by the excessive flow when upstream dams burst. Had she lived, she would have been forced to give birth in the open, making her and her babies vulnerable.

The trapper couldn't bring the mother beaver back to life, but thought he might be able to give her babies a chance. He immediately performed a crude Caesarean section on the dead female. He gently removed three tiny kit beavers, still alive, all perfect little replicas of their mom. He wrapped them in his shirt to keep them warm and then he headed home.

Wild young have a hard time surviving the harsh realities of their natural world, even when an experienced mom tends to them and they have received strength and immunities from her care and nourishment. All mammal mothers produce special milk for their babies during the first few days of suckling. Much thicker in consistency than normal milk, it contains what babies need to develop and build their immune systems. However, these kits were to have no such inoculation.

Shannon and her family presented me with a small container, padded, soft and clean, with three tiny fuzzy beavers. Their greyish-brown fur looked like fleece or thick felt, and their tiny features, feet, and tails were ridiculously cute and perfect. Their cries were of hunger, but not pain or distress, and although not fat, they seemed well hydrated. There was evidence of diarrhea on the kits' bedding, but not so much that I was overly concerned.

My first task was to take the baby beavers home, warm, feed, and house them in a darkened environment. They had already been introduced to a human baby's bottle and nipple. They found the nipple large and awkward in their tiny mouths, but they each managed to feed a bit. It was not my intent to fill their tummies right away. This can often cause terrible bloating and pain to a baby, especially if a new food is introduced in large amounts. The method I used with the young beavers was the one I used successfully with other orphans to get them to accept a strange formula. I fed them initially with electrolytes, then with an electrolyte/formula mixture. Finally, I switched them onto a full-strength formula suggested in rehabilitation publications on animal nutrition as suitable for young beavers. This took a day or so, as their stomachs had to adjust to the new food. Once they had received full-strength formula for several feedings and their stools seemed to be relatively normal, I added small amounts of probiotics to their food, to help to build up the gut bacteria required for digesting food and absorbing nutrients.

The kits' weights ranged from 300 to 485 grams when I first received them. I have to admit that at the time, I didn't hold out much hope for the littlest one. The other two seemed to be growing daily, but the smallest was slow to develop. He would continually fall asleep while eating. I tickled and coaxed him constantly, just to get him to swallow a few mouthfuls of formula.

The first two beaver orphans I had raised a few years back were accustomed to passing their body wastes into water and would do so as they floated in the tub. These new little beavers did not seem to have the buoyancy that Eh and Bea had. Possibly because of their Caesarean birth, their lungs were not as fully developed as those of naturally born kits. As a result, these little newcomers could not be placed in tub water for the purpose of elimination without sinking beneath the surface. Instead, when it came time for them to go about their body functions, I applied a wet, soft cloth very gently in the appropriate area. That seemed to do the trick.

Mostly, the kits slept.

Deep in slumber, they sought comfort by sucking on each other's ears or their own tails, all the while curled up like large fuzzy cutworms. The littlest one took the brunt of the ear sucking. Each of the larger siblings would attach themselves to one of his ears at night, and fall asleep despite the little one's struggles and protests. It wasn't long before the hair on his silky little shell-shaped ears slipped right off. If I heard his cries of indignation, I would go in to detach the siblings. I used this as an excuse to hold him for a few minutes until the other two fell asleep. I'd have to laugh at his appearance on these occasions, as his poor little brown beaver ears would be all slick and tufted up on the top with slobber. All that was missing from this punk look was body piercing!

I was afraid he would get ear infections from the constant moisture and formula that stuck to them, not to mention the fact it obviously distressed him. I couldn't use any deterring substances that would hurt or sicken him or his siblings, but felt compelled to try to find something that would work. I tried everything I could think of to stop his siblings from their overbearing attentions to his ear. I made earmuffs of painter tape that were soon pulled off. I even went as far as separating them, but that was too stressful and they wouldn't settle to sleep until they were all together again. A strong-smelling cold ointment won out, and its bitter camphor taste seemed to hold the little ear-suckers at bay. However, the tiny ears of the smallest beaver had become chapped and infected from the constant attention.

All wrapped up in his own sorrow, the little one would focus on sucking his own tail, but seemed to gain little comfort from it, for he would still occasionally squeal in anger when a sibling sucked or nipped his tender raw ears. I had to remain diligent with the ointment. I didn't realize the intensity of his sucking habit until I noticed a large, blood-filled embolism forming on the tip of his tail. To this day, a circular chunk missing from the tip of his tail serves as a remembrance of his self-mutilation. If his siblings were sucking that hard, too, I'm surprised he didn't end up earless.

Not too long after taking in the beaver kits, I returned to my desk one day after working in the field, and found several brightly coloured notes stuck to my chair, computer, and door. The front office staff obviously wanted to make sure I checked with them before I left to go home. I walked to the front of the office, where I noticed several sets of concerned eyes focused on a cardboard carton stowed under a desk. The box seemed to be bouncing. Out of the top of the box popped a long black neck and head that wobbled back and forth. Dark, shiny eyes stared back at my co-workers with matched curiosity and surprise. A gosling, nearly the same age as Janice but with fuller, more complete plumage, "wee-wee-ed" a greeting as I approached.

"Lucky," the note attached to her cardboard carton explained, had been picked up near the northern community of Weagamow Lake, after one or both of its parents were killed. A young woman had kept Lucky alive and well-fed, but she was afraid for its safety. Both domestic and wild canids—dogs and foxes—had free range in the community and she wasn't sure that she could protect the goose as it grew. Lucky's bad luck was Janice's good fortune! She now had company to grow with.

When I introduced the two goslings to each other at home that evening, I felt a great sense of hope for their future. I watched the two geese interact and realized that humans like me would no longer be the focus of their lives. They immediately clung to each other, twining their necks across each other's back when resting. If one preened its feathers, so did the other.

After Lucky and Janice finished their introductions and social interactions, they started to walk around the yard, feeding. Then Lucky spotted the pond, and excitedly flip-flopped her way to the water's edge and started to feed. Janice followed excitedly, head and neck down. "Weee weee weee," she went, all the way down the slope. She had never made this journey without me before, so I watched nervously from the balcony for signs of the hunting goshawk or bald eagles that frequented the pond. As I watched, an eagle started flying tight circles above the pond; still just a speck in the evening sky, but working its way down. I glanced back down to the pond, but I saw no sign of the goslings, just ripples leading to the shore. I grabbed my binoculars, and scanned the tall sedges. It took a few frantic moments before I saw the silhouettes of both goslings, lying flat and motionless in the thick grass, heads flat on the ground. They stayed this way for the better part of an hour, long after the eagle moved on to another hunting spot. This was another example of innate behaviour, a response to a predator without training from a parent or life experience. It was definitely a lesson I could never have taught them, and fortunately, didn't have to.

Joining forces gave the goslings more security because now they could watch out for each other, one feeding while the other remained on the lookout for predators. This new independence allowed them to increase their access to the plethora of grasses, seeds, invertebrates, and mineral-rich clays in the pond. It also gave me extra time to deal with some issues that were happening with the young beaver kits, so I was frequently able to leave the little geese alone to fend for themselves. They weren't totally without a lifeline, though. I set up baby monitors near the shore so I could hear their distress calls. I hoped I would be able to reach them before anything terrible happened to them.

It soon became apparent that the beaver kits still had digestive problems. They continued to act colicky and their stools remained runny and odoriferous. Despite my restricting their diet to a goat's-milk-based puppy formula and adding commercially prepared probiotics, their little systems simply were not working the way they should. The company that had made the standard orphan puppy formula I used when raising Eh and Bea had changed its formula. The new recipe seemed to have been the cause of terrible problems in young squirrels and groundhogs I had fed it to, things like clouded eyes, yeast-like skin infections, and severe hair loss. However, another commercially produced formula, derived from goat's milk, had seemed to be more agreeable to the small mammals I had fed it to. So I switched the formula I fed to the beavers, but kept their feedings small and frequent. Then I hoped that the new diet would agree with their digestive systems. The change seemed to reduce the bloating and cramps they were prone to, especially after a substantial feeding, while I felt it still ensured they were getting sufficient nutrition.

The kits' frequent feedings cut in on any free time I had and even some of my not-so-free time. It helped that the goslings remained together feeding themselves on the pond, which lessened my workload somewhat, but there were other wards in my care that also needed attention. Often, I felt burnt out, and questioned whether rehabilitation as I practised it was really a hobby.

I gratefully accepted offers by visiting friends to oversee the beavers while they were playing and exercising in their outside enclosure. I was quick with instructions as to what was required, and with reminders of no human contact unless in an emergency, my volunteers willingly took on the many tasks required to raise the beaver kits. Even if their role was just to watch for danger or escapees while the kits swam or played outside, it freed up my time for my other wards. I don't think they minded these tasks too much though, as the kits were so endearing. In fact, I'm pretty sure I saw a tear or two well up in their eyes, especially when they helped feed the little creatures. When a tiny paw would close around their pinky finger, gripping tightly while they nursed on their bottle, I could see their emotions surface. For all of us, observing the little kits in their helpless innocence was indeed a heartwarming experience.

But despite the care, nurturing, and love, I sensed the kits were struggling to survive. The mid-sized one just wasn't progressing as she should. She had entered this world prematurely and her little organs hadn't developed properly, or somehow weren't strong enough without the food and nutrition from a real mother. No amount of food or care from a surrogate could change what was to be. One morning, still curled up tightly with her brothers, she didn't wake up. Her siblings did not seem to notice she had left them when I freed her still-warm little body from the furry tangle.

I gave Shannon an update on the kits, sadly breaking the news about losing one of them. She hesitantly asked about the littlest one, whom I found out her family had developed a particular soft spot for in the short time they cared for them. I had to tell her I believed he was just barely hanging in, unlike the biggest kit, who was now starting to grow in leaps and bounds, by all appearances robust and healthy.

I believe that a name gives its bearer strength and purpose, so I asked Shannon if her family had thought of names for the kits. I could use the names as reference when we spoke of them. She said that her children liked the names Cameron and Hunny. So it was to be. Cameron, a tiny little thing given such a big name to live up to, and his sibling Hunny, who still seemed strong, were so named.

I continued with their care, adjusting and adding to their diet as required, all the while hoping for the best. I was encouraged as the pair seemed to be over the worst of their digestive crisis, but the one-sided growth trend continued. Hunny was outsizing his brother in leaps and bounds. He continued to bully him and suck on Cameron's ear when he slept. Despite the size difference, both could now take their bottle in their own paws, and while lying on their sides or tummy, collapse the plastic sides of the bottle with their enthusiastic suckling. Things were looking up!

Meanwhile, the goslings were growing quickly too and were constantly preening the drying, flaking sheaths off their new feathers. Lucky's feathers seemed to be developing nicely and he could even take short test flights. Janice's wings, however, were causing me some concern. The long flight feathers were growing too fast for the developing wing bones. The weight of the large primaries seemed to be causing her wings to droop and the wingtips to drag when she was tired.

I read up on similar cases and after checking with my friends at the vet clinic, we came to the conclusion that I had been too indulgent to Janice when she was an only gosling. She had loved cat kibble and other prepared food I had initially fed her, so when I was in too much of a hurry to pick the large amount of fresh grass she needed to see her through the day, I would give her a big bowl of kibble and grain to tide her over. This high-protein diet must have caused an imbalance in bone growth as opposed to feather growth. Her flight feathers grew too quickly and were too heavy for the soft bones and growing tendons to support. Once the problem had been identified, I tried to rectify the situation by increasing her calcium and phosphorous intake, hoping she would grow into her feathers. I also fastened her wings into their proper position with a hair clip at night. This eased the tension on the weak muscles, holding her growing bone joints in proper position while keeping the new feathers clean.

But by morning, Lucky would have the offending hair clip groomed from Janice's back. I, or I guess I should say we, kept up this routine for some time, until I came up with a plan. With a bit of glue and some molted goose feathers, I camouflaged the clip, using just enough glue to attach the feathers on the clip, while ensuring they lay flat along the wing. I knew if they stuck up at all on Janice's back, either she or Lucky would preen them off. The next morning, the clip was still in place, and remained so every night afterwards. And its effects were long-lasting. For days the wing stayed in place, seemingly better each day, as the geese continued to swim and feed in the pond.

The beaver kits were also starting to enjoy their swims along the shore of the pond and no longer protested getting wet. They responded eagerly to natural foods, such as algae, leaves, and grasses, humming contentedly while they ate. I didn't realize just how important it was at the time, but Cameron started to eat mud and dirt, just as the moose calf had. Then his tastes changed from gross to disgusting, as I saw Cameron eating what I realized too late was fecal matter from the pond's resident beavers. There was a chance this copraphagic behaviour could introduce parasites or bacteria that his compromised immune system couldn't fight. I can't be sure, but contrary to my worst fears, this stuff seemed to really help and not hurt him. Thinking back, it would likely have helped Hunny too, if only he had indulged in the predigested goop. Eating mud and feces introduced natural biotics and trace minerals into Cameron's digestive system, allowing it to develop and function normally. While hindsight is twenty-twenty, this is too often little consolation. For example, remembering my past experiences with baby hares, the moose calf, and what I observed with Cameron, I may have been able to prevent problems in Hunny, the larger beaver kit, had I been more forceful in my encouragement.

Young snowshoe hares are common wards at wildlife centres. They are painfully cute, tiny and easy to catch, and as a result are frequently rescued by human bunny-nappers. Stress from handling as well as the inevitable cow's milk meal they receive before they are delivered to experienced caregivers like myself, cause extreme bloat and pain to the youngsters. Literature on successful rehabilitation of young snowshoe hares recommends taking fresh morning droppings of adult hares or rabbits, which are in soft, grapelike clusters, or even the stomach contents of a fresh road-killed hare, and adding this to the babies' food to reduce digestion problems. The natural bacteria released from the adult's gut and droppings help to kick-start the little ones' digestive systems. I think the same principle applies to most other wild animals, and I now know it applies to beavers.

It seems that Cameron innately knew this when he ate the feces in the pond, and his copraphagia and geophagy seemed to be the turning point in his development. I think I was able to notice the difference within a day or two. The biggest change was that he soon had very little body odour. Hunny, meanwhile, still smelled of sour, poorly digested formula, despite his baths and clean surroundings. I had wondered about this rancid scent they carried, as I remembered that Eh and Bea, while fed similar diets, smelled so sweet and clean. A healthy young animal should not emit a noticeable odour.

It made sense that the sour fetor being emitted by Hunny was from formula that his little system was fighting to digest. Cameron, almost sweet-smelling now, had obviously reacted positively to his pond-bottom browsing, and was digesting without problems. I hoped Hunny would follow suit. Despite my encouragement to eat some scum by offering him the same natural elements that Cameron had consumed, smeared on foods familiar to Hunny, he would remove the offending material from his mouth with a swipe of his paw and an accusatory whine.

I will never know for sure if my hasty rescue one day of the beaver kits amplified Hunny's digestive woes, but the end result was tragic. It happened as I stood and watched as the kits played and fed in a small, shaded, grassy pool upstream of the main pond. Amused by their antics, I was oblivious to the approach of a very large black bear until he started heading our way, and was closing in fast. His nose was in the air, indicating to me he had scented a potential food source. Bears are omnivores, which means they can and will eat just about anything. However, they are known to be especially fond of the flesh of beavers. Normally a bear would be frightened by human presence, but the chance at an easy meal seemed to be too much for the bruin to turn down. My options raced through my head, and although my first impulse was to run for safety and hope he didn't find the kits, I knew running could provoke an attack. Plus I couldn't leave the helpless little mites by themselves. But my movements were rushed and jerky, and frightened the little beavers as I lurched over to grab them.

When I gathered the two baby beavers up, I didn't have time to support them in my arms properly. I was able to scoop up Cameron safely into his little carrying basket, but Hunny was made nervous by my frantic movements and swam out of reach. I splashed after him and gripped him around the middle as he squirmed to get away, unable to give his tummy and body proper support. I felt his weight sagging into my hands as I lifted him from the buoyancy of the water, and he whined uncomfortably. I set him into the basket with Cameron and quickly skirted the edge of the field, keeping my eye on the approaching bear. I saw it stop. It stood and sniffed the air, whuffing as he caught human scent. He sniffed the air again, and slowly moved away, checking over his shoulder as he retreated into the woods, his fear of humans overruling his hunger.

A beaver's body shape is ideal for floating and swimming. Beneath their fur and skin sheets of muscle support their internal organs. Huge coils of intestines are intricately looped in the body cavity below a large liver. The ribs that enclose the heart and lungs are quite thin and flexible. Picking a beaver up off the ground, without proper support, can cause the ribs to push into the liver and the intestines to push and fold on each other in a manner they should not. If their stomach is full of food, torsion in the gut may occur, causing a twist or telescoping that will not easily correct itself. This is not unlike what happens in some large dog breeds when they are fed just one big meal a day. Gorging, followed by vigorous activity, can cause the animal's intestines, heavy with food, to loop or twist, presenting a potentially fatal condition. When I grabbed up Hunny, this might have happened to him.

Once they were safely back in their enclosure, both kits started grooming their ruffled, wet fur. While Hunny's grooming behaviour and movements seemed normal and he made no further fuss and showed no further discomfort at that time, I think this was when his health started to seriously deteriorate. That evening, after his meal, Hunny whined for his bathroom. I put him in the tub, but instead of the immediate relief it should have allowed him, only a bit of air passed out of his system. He arched his back and groaned. A bit of back rubbing resulted in the release of tummy gases, and he seemed marginally better. Instead of his typical grooming and drying after being in the tub, he sat, appearing to be dazed. I dried him carefully with a soft towel and put him into his bed where he fell into a fitful sleep. The next day's feeding brought the same reaction.

While I was in the midst of administering to the ailing kit, friends had popped in to visit. I put them to work, instructing them to keep Cameron occupied while I tried to settle Hunny down. It was as if he had colic and, like a human child, would stretch backwards, moaning. I was very upset when I couldn't provide him relief. I tried gentle warming of his tummy, back rubs and a bit of ginger water to calm his tummy. Nothing worked.

I made a panicked call to the vet clinic. After listening to my account of Hunny's condition, Dr. Christiansen agreed that I should bring him in immediately. There was no evidence that his tummy had twisted, but some of the symptoms he showed suggested he might be suffering from Tyzzer's disease, a common and treatable condition affecting the rodent family. We stressed him further during these tests, but it had to be done. After a short and anxious wait, the results were in… the blood samples were negative for Tyzzer's. We were at a loss. Sedatives and antibiotics were administered to allow him some relief and possibly combat the unknown. We could only wait and hope. I took him home and settled him into a padded box beside my bed where I could lie with my warm hand on his little body to comfort him. I was to get no sleep that night. Hunny managed some restless sleep. He showed signs of cramps, arching his little back and sighing, relaxing slightly when I applied a gentle backrub.

That night, as I lay in the darkness, unable to sleep, mulling over possible causes and cures for Hunny, I suddenly realized that he had not had a significant bowel movement in two days. I had forgotten to mention that fact when we were examining him at the clinic. It was possible, even likely, his discomfort was from a blockage in his intestines. If this were the case, then poisons were building up in his body. But there was nothing I could do until the morning. Perhaps my vet would know what more could be done. As I anxiously waited the dawn, I observed Hunny had become less fitful in his troubled sleep. I hoped that it was the effects of the antibiotics helping him feel better, but that was not the case. He passed away in his troubled sleep, his tiny little body rigid in his discomfort.

A necropsy later confirmed that his intestines had folded over on themselves and had not been able to function normally. They had atrophied, spreading infection throughout his body. I felt so badly for him. Although Dr. Christiansen assured me that his premature birth and underdeveloped system was likely the cause of his demise, I continued to blame myself for my hasty rescue of Hunny when the bear scared me.

As I cleaned and sterilized the beaver's living quarters, I realized how small and vulnerable the remaining kit appeared as it lay snoozing in its fresh, clean bedding. If Cameron's larger brother and sister could not survive this world, Cameron's chances were even more doubtful. But I knew that I had to keep trying. His little mumbles and burbles as he sucked his tail were those of a contented soul. He seemed not to mind that his bedmate now was a stuffed toy beaver. At least this roommate was not fixated on his ears, was soft, dry, and sweet-smelling, and would lie with him, quietly and companionably. All the while, Cameron continued his own bad habit of sucking on the tip of his tail.

Although this was not the case with Hunny, the living body can sometimes be very forgiving and will heal itself if given time, opportunity, and proper nutrition. As further proof of this, about two weeks into her fortified diet, Janice the gosling started testing her wings, able to hold them out without any drooping or apparent weakness. She was as delighted as I was and would flap so hard her feet would leave the ground. Both the young geese now had adult feathering, except for the occasional downy yellow tuft sticking out of their glossy black heads. Together they practised short flights around the pond. They swam to the highest beaver dam, walked to a flat, elevated area, then preened, stretched, and flapped with such fury that they would lift right off the ground. After going through this ritual warmup, they would launch themselves into the air with a great to-do.

Judging from all the noise they made during their initial flights, I am certain they began their airborne career thinking that honking was just as critical to maintaining altitude as flapping. However, the need to employ other, finer points of flight seemed to be lacking. After several end-over-end tumbles, a few episodes of running out of runway and bushing themselves in the trees, and several aborted landings, they started to fine-tune their aerobatics. Soon they learned to launch, glide, and then put their feet down to splash to a halt. Each practice run ended with them greeting each other with heads-down "wee wee weeing" their comments and criticisms on the other's technique.

The fledgling geese were energetic feeders, and as the pond beavers slowly raised the water levels and new patches of sedges were flooded, the geese moved in and uprooted the mats in search of tender greens and bugs. Three mallard broods and a green-winged teal family nesting near the pond benefited from the goslings' excavations, too. They learned to wait their turn, to avoid the hissy fits the young geese used to drive them off if they tried to muscle in too close. The larger-bodied geese would excavate an area in the muddy bottom, eating their fill of aquatic plants before moving on down the shore. Then the young duck families would rush into the newly excavated area, searching for food and eagerly eating the tiny invertebrates and plant seeds the geese had left behind.

The pond was noisy with wildlife sounds most mornings and evenings, but during the midday all was strangely silent. The transposition from a busy, occupied, feeding ground to a calm, quiet, presumably deserted pond was swift and efficient as morning turned to day. With the aid of binoculars, I witnessed just how the quiet exodus occurred. The family of baby teal slipped under an overturned root, while mom flew off through the tree, under the radar, so to speak, of watchful predators. The older mallard brood, nearly fully feathered, lined up on a sun-kissed log to preen, while a more recent hatch of mallards, the young brood still covered in down, disappeared into a brush pile on the shore. The young geese disappeared silently into the long grass. A shiny, black bill seen pecking at a seed pod gave away their position. Hawks and eagles, using the warming midday thermals to soar silently, would be hard-pressed to find a meal from these waters. Come evening, the pond residents would materialize again and start their feeding frenzy anew. The order in which the waterfowl departed the pond each day may have slightly varied, but the activity continued into the summer until the ducklings were feathered and almost fully grown.

Cameron seemed to be doing okay without benefit of his siblings. He certainly didn't seem to mind that he no longer had a larger sibling climbing on his back giving him a snootful of water and interrupting his swims. And his ears started to heal, no longer coated with sticky formula and slobbers. Maybe there is something to be said about being an only child.

By now I was positive his earlier ingesting of fecal matter from the adult beavers in the pond had done him good. An old proverb says that we will all eat a peck of dirt before we die. Seems there might be some truth in these sayings.

Cameron's steady growth was heartening. And he was showing a new *joie de vivre*. He wanted to play and swim in the big beaver pond more and more. When I put him out for exercise, I watched him carefully, for in the wink of an eye he would romp down the hill and into the deep water where I couldn't reach him. The large swimming pool was not interesting enough for him anymore. If he made it to the beaver pond, there would usually be a merry chase through the mud, sedges, and turbid waters. He seemed to enjoy these little ventures and treated them like play. He willingly crawled into his little carrying basket when he tired of the game, and would happily groom the mud out of his fur as I carried him up the hill.

I could let him in the big pond only when the resident beavers were in their houses for the day or feeding on the far edge of the pond. Sometimes they came out early to feed, and their contact calls intrigued Cameron to investigate. Since resident beavers can be violent with trespassers, I needed to wade out in the muck and guck to convince him to climb into his basket, or else risk him becoming a furry beaver chew.

He needed some kind of protective pen where he could swim and dig and feed in the big pond he loved, without the danger of being attacked by the adult beavers. Strength, height, energy, and having only two arms had all been limiting factors in my past construction attempts. I knew I would need to seek help for this project, and I had an idea of where I could tap into an energetic, willing, and able workforce.

With that prospect in mind, I purchased a large dog-run kit from a local hardware store. The structure I bought was light enough that I could lift and move it around by myself. It had no floor or roof, which served my purpose fine. The kennel wire would not give way too easily to the trying teeth of the adult beavers. And it was large enough (six feet by six feet by twelve feet), to allow ample room for Cameron to swim and play. Now, to check on that workforce...

The Ontario Ministry of Natural Resources was sponsoring an Ontario Stewardship Rangers program in Kenora. Assisting me at my wildlife rehabilitation centre had been a favourite project for the young rangers the previous year, so they had already slotted in a day this season for helping me out. I was able to book a vacation day so that I could be there to supervise and enjoy the enthusiastic crew's banter as they worked.

There were problems, though, at the beginning.

It seems all my construction projects have hitches. The pouring rain was only a minor annoyance. When we unpacked the pen, we found it was missing several critical components. This was a major annoyance. I made a frantic call to the hardware store, pleading my case, blubbering about a lost vacation day and explaining my limited access to a labour force. "Time is of the essence," I pleaded.

Within the hour, the store manager himself delivered a new, unopened kennel package to my door. Psyched up once more, the girls unpacked the new box. More problems were obvious when we put it to use. While the new package had some of the missing parts, an essential extension wasn't there, plus the length of wire was two feet short. No fault of the local store manager, it seemed the inspector at the manufacturer had been asleep at the helm, waking only long enough to defiantly leave his inspector's number in the packaging. Fortunately, there were odds and sods of kennel wiring in our garage, left over after the construction of my raptor flight cages in past years. These bits and pieces of wire were able to serve our purpose.

By the time my workers had to pack up to leave, the skies had cleared, I had a baby beaver habitat, the rangers had a sense of resourcefulness and accomplishment, and we all had great respect for the store manager who saved the day.

Cameron seemed thrilled with the independence his new enclosure gave him. I, too, had obtained a new level of independence and figured I could now leave him to play in his pen while I worked around the yard.

The first day though, I thought I was seeing things when I looked up from my yard work to see the pen some eight or ten feet from where I had first set it up. My first thought was that a bear had pushed it to get at the beaver. I raced up to the high balcony to check things out.

From my vantage point on the balcony, I observed what looked like a tiny little bathtub toy churning up the mud inside the pen. It was Cameron, paddling for all he was worth, trying to push the bottom rail of the pen out of the depression it was stuck in. It seems he discovered that as long as the pen was sitting on a spot where the bottom of the pond was smooth and hard, he was strong enough to push his new habitat around. The hollow aluminum bars along the bottom of the pen held air pockets, adding a bit of buoyancy. When Cameron pushed in a certain spot, one side of the pen would lift off the bottom with the trapped air collecting on the high side, allowing that side to float. Once floating, he was off and running (or paddling).

Later that day, I ruined his fun by pinning the rails into the mud. He still hadn't developed the ability to dive underwater for more than a few seconds, so he didn't try to dig underneath. Those diving skills would develop later, but for now, I could relax.

By late August, the geese were strong flyers, winging off to unknown destinations after their morning treat of grain. I often would see them fly down the valley alongside my vehicle as I left for work, before they would veer off, possibly to a nearby lake or farmer's field frequented by other geese. I did not know from day to day if they would return. While they wouldn't likely be migrating for a while—at least as long as the fall remained mild—they would be as vulnerable to goose hunters as the wild populations were. When goose season opened on the first of September, my anxiety level increased. Each day I would fret until I saw the pair of winged wanderers land back on my pond, safe for another day.

There is a strange paradox in our human population. I have had people who regularly hunt for waterfowl pick up and bring to me injured waterfowl they have found, even during the hunting season. It seems that in the eyes of the people who find them, these birds are not considered fair and legal game if they were not hunting at the time, so they do not try to claim them as part of their legal bag limit. While some folks may still dispatch a critically injured bird and add it to their daily bag and their freezer, oddly enough many will not, at least not if the injuries appear slight. Instead, they bring them to me for repairs. Therefore it is common for me, during the fall months, to receive phone calls from the vet clinic informing me that someone has brought in a duck or goose with stray shot in it, and could I come pick it up? So when such a call came from Paula, one of the clinic staff, I didn't find it so unusual. And when she called, she wanted my reassurance that I would do my best for this particular bird.

"Lil, it seems like such a nice goose, and it actually seems to like us," she said.

Normally, a Canada goose will nip and pinch with great gusto any piece of anatomy it can reach. I was surprised this one had spared the ladies at the clinic such nasty treatment.

As I entered the busy waiting room, Paula waved me to the back room of the clinic. A kennel isolated from recuperating pets sat there, and from it a long, sleek black neck snaked out as I approached. A set of beady, black eyes stared fearlessly at me. As I walked up to the goose, now standing defiantly in the kennel, I noted the wings had a slight droop, an artifact from her nutrition deficit problem as a gosling. When I opened the door of the kennel, the goose immediately shoved her head under my hair and started to nibble my neck. A small purple band I had placed on her leg confirmed her identity. The rescued goose was Janice.

Shotgun pellets could have made the small puncture wounds and scratches that dotted her flesh and skin. Then again, an eagle's talon could have made a similar pattern. Sore and scared but otherwise safe, she readily came to me, allowing me to load her into a carrier. Janice dozed on the trip home, tucking her head under her wing for most of the trip, jumping nervously from time to time as if awaking from some horrible nightmare. When I released her back to the familiar surroundings of the pond, she obviously wasn't her old self.

It was so strange to see her alone. She had followed Lucky everywhere from the very first day they were introduced. Except now there was no Lucky. Instead of spending her time down at the pond, as a contented goose should, she sat on my deck, head and neck positioned across her back. Every once in a while she would emit a long, sad-sounding "huu-onk," or tilt up her head to stare hopefully at a flock of passing geese. Then she would settle again, despondent.

As the week passed, she ate just enough food to keep up her strength. She made no attempt to fly or go down to the pond for a bath or swim. Her muscles were becoming soft and her wing droop more pronounced. I wondered if perhaps her injuries were causing her to be so lethargic, even though they had not seemed to be life threatening. The treat of grain I would leave with her was, more often than not, still beside her and untouched when I returned from work.

One morning, as I walked past her on the deck where she maintained her vigil, I noticed she was becoming increasingly agitated. She started calling excitedly, pacing back and forth. I could hear a faint goose call in the distance. It was fall and there were many flocks flying south. I didn't pay much attention to the sound, other than to appreciate its haunting beauty. While the goose call didn't strike me as unusual, Janice's behaviour did. She was now standing, flapping her wings frantically. I looked down to the pond just in time to see two Canada geese land in a flurry of splashing and flapping and excited calls. One of the newcomers started waddling up the hill to the house as Janice flapped her way down to meet it.

The second newcomer, an unfamiliar adult, stayed at the pond's edge, leery of my presence and that of the loud, excited youngster, while the juvenile ran, head down, to greet Janice. They did their introductions, heads down and "wee-wee-weeing" gleefully at each other. They then strolled side by side, uttering excited little calls, to join the adult at the pond's edge. I couldn't believe it could be Lucky, but it was, as the corresponding purple band visible on his leg proved. And somehow, he had picked up an adult chaperone in his travels. I was really happy with the turn of events but, it seems, every silver lining has a cloud.

# Sad Days Ahead

When I went to work the next day, excited to share the story of the geese, I was greeted by sombre faces. One of my co-workers quietly informed me that a friend of mine, the local animal control officer for the City of Kenora, had suddenly passed away, leaving a young family and many, many friends to grieve his passing. Over the years, Mike had become my friend and ally in the care and rescue of wildlife found or hurt within the city limits. He valued all wildlife, from a bedraggled raven pulled out of a restaurant's grease pit to young pigeons spray-painted in gang colours and left to fend for themselves in a deserted parking lot. A big part of his job had been to live-trap and move nuisance bears. And this particular year, he had moved them by the dozens, all the while treating them with respect. He loved the bears despite the long, hard hours of work they created. It had been a poor year for berry crops, and the bears had moved to town en masse looking for easy food.

I would miss his "Lil, guess what I have for you." With Mike it could have been any species, any size, in any predicament.

As I walked into our house after attending his funeral, I mused that sometimes life just isn't fair. The dogs immediately sensed my mood and were squirmy and obsequious, trying to cheer me up with their antics. Taking them for a swim or a good long walk was the solution to my blue mood, but I just wanted to sulk for a while. I left them sitting expectantly on the step with their leashes in their mouths, while I went to the garage to check on Cameron.

For once, Cameron actually seemed excited to see me, and he raised his arms in the "uppy, uppy" position. This was new. Eh had often asked to be picked up, but Cameron hadn't. As I lifted him up, he snuggled under my chin and gripped my fingers in his paws. He lay there quietly against my torso, puffing his sweet breath onto my neck. We sat companionably like this for a good while. Our reverie was finally broken when the dogs, tired of waiting, pounded on the garage door, whining their impatience. Sufficiently consoled, I returned Cameron to his bed, and escorted the dogs on a long walk. There is nothing like a good, warm hug to soothe the soul, whether from man or beast.

If only I could have bottled up that good feeling. I would have need of it in the weeks that followed.

The Labour Day long weekend of September was upon me and I had things to do. This is the weekend I slate into my schedule every fall to get the pens and facilities cleaned and patched for the fall migration and its rush of new patients. Autumn is the season when young, migrating hawks and waterfowl either run out of steam, venture too low over a highway, or get hit by stray pellets with the opening of hunting season. I had gratefully accepted an offer of help with these chores from a friend from work. She knew what needed doing and could work on one project, while I tackled another. Plus she would provide cheery company, making the work seem almost fun. When Christy called, apologizing that she had to cancel, I was kind of bummed out.

As I prepared to tackle some of the more pressing tasks by myself, I looked up to see a car in the driveway. A friend who owned a cottage nearby stood by her vehicle with a beatific grin on her face. She was struggling under the weight of a large plastic tub that was slopping water from its rim as she balanced it. She had left her friends and family at their nearby cottage making breakfast, in order to deliver to me (or rather to Cameron) a large tub full of lily roots. She explained that the nearby beaver lodge had oodles of these roots floating around it, dug up by the local beavers. Remembering how much Eh had liked them, she had collected some for Cameron. After selecting a few choice pieces, we took them to Cameron and watched as he excitedly handled each piece. With an excited "whee" he chewed into the tough covering, discovering the tasty fibres within.

"Oh, Lil, he is so sweet," she whispered. "I'm so glad he is doing well. Last time I saw him, he was little and feeble. You said then you didn't think he would live more than a few days."

We watched a few moments more, then moved out into the sunlight, leaving Cameron to his breakfast. She asked what my plans were for the day. When I told her what they had been and how they had been altered somewhat, she offered to help out with some of the jobs that required two. We laboured side by side, enjoying each other's company and chatting as we worked

Once the largest part of the lifting and toting was taken care of, I felt guilty taking up her time when she should be visiting with her friends at the cottage. After we moved the last heavy roll of kennel wire into storage, I walked her back to her car. We stood for few minutes with the chickens pecking and scratching around our feet and talked, mostly about the beautiful day it had turned out to be. I thanked her for her help and offered the freshly laid eggs from my hens to replace her missed breakfast.

As she climbed into the car, egg carton in hand, she smiled and said, "You know, Lil, there are only so many beautiful days like this left … you should kick back and enjoy it instead of working so hard."

She's right, winter will be here soon enough, I thought.

I followed her suggestion and took my time finishing a few of the less onerous tasks. Then I enjoyed the rest of the day, walking the dogs and enjoying the beauty of the season. I had no way of knowing that when we said goodbye that morning, it would be the last sunny day we would share. Later that week, I received news of her untimely death.

I've been accused of being forever an optimist, believing it's always darkest before the dawn, every cloud has a silver lining and all that pep-talk stuff. In retrospect, I can admit now that September 2001 held some of the darkest, saddest moments of my life. Losing two good friends, both so young and vital, filled me with a great sorrow. I found I had to work hard to keep my sadness in control. I focused on my job, avoiding conversations with co-workers whenever possible, while trying to always remain polite. I seemed to be constantly on the brink of tears, and driving past my friend's cottage every day on my way home would bring a new flood of emotions. Bruce was only home on weekends, so at least he wasn't constantly faced with my roller-coaster emotions. My movements around the yard feeding, watering, and exercising my wards were robotic and restrained. The unseasonably warm fall helped matters somewhat, and there were very few new patients coming in to the centre, giving me some badly needed respite. I focused on rehabilitating those already in my care and on getting myself out of my deep funk.

The geese no longer needed my care and they spent a further month or so at the beaver pond, feeding and swimming under the guidance of the adult chaperone. The adult maintained a respectful distance from me, and would scold the youngsters whenever they approached me. All three would eat the grain and corn I left, but I knew I once again had to wean the youngsters from the supplementary feedings. Their flights had started again, and as before, they would sometimes be gone for days. While I worried about what fate they might encounter, I was no longer concerned whether they would have the instinct to migrate. The adult had obviously taken charge and because it was a seasoned migrant I was confident it would teach the young ones the ropes.

Wildlife behaviours described in books are not always black-and-white facts in spite of what wildlife experts may say. There are definitely exceptions. We have so much more to learn about even something as common as a goose. Here was a case of two imprinted geese that, despite being raised by me, allowed themselves to be taken under the wing, so to speak, of a wild adult. They readily followed it, fed with it, and seemed willing to follow it south. I suppose the true test of their success would be for them to return to the pond in their second year. As yearling birds, they would return to the north later than the paired adults, who come early to check out nesting sites. If all went well in the south, Janice and Lucky would arrive back here as molt migrants with other yearlings and laze around, without going through the process of breeding. It is during the second year of their life when pair bonds are established.

Allowing Cameron to be out where he could have contact by smell, sound, and even sight with other beavers, while still providing him some level of protection, was an important step in his independence, too. This little beaver never knew his mother, and never seemed to have bonded with his siblings. When they died, he didn't seem to notice their absence. When raising Eh and Bea, I couldn't help but notice how they had bonded to each other. I remember the heartbreaking moments I had with Eh when Bea died. When his brother and sister died, Cameron hadn't expressed any sign of recognizable emotion or, for that matter, any indication that he noticed them gone.

Now that he was safely ensconced in his aquatic pen, I could watch his interaction with the pond beavers. Having determined that they could not get rid of Cameron, the adults seemed to ignore him. Initially, they had circled this strange structure and its unfamiliar inhabitant, and there had been much in the way of huffs, hisses, and tail slaps. But that had been it, and now they seemed to be interested only in going about their business.

The pond's young wild beavers, though, would continue to visit him. Despite the adult beavers' warnings, they would line up in front of the pen. When they gathered up enough courage, they would swim underwater, popping up, still outside the pen, uttering little "whee"s and wheezes. They would float back and forth parallel to Cameron's movements. Cameron watched with interest, followed their movements, and would usually return their calls for a while before returning to his ongoing in-pen habitat alterations, ignoring his visitors.

The aquatic pen system worked great for daytime play. Cameron still spent the night safe in his cardboard container in the garage. Because he was growing steadily, he now required refrigerator-sized boxes. I would lay the box on its side, then line it with newspaper and straw, with a smaller-sized box in one end acting as a lodge. In the other end of the large box, there was still room for a large galvanized tub of water. When I was home and available to watch for bears, he could spend time in the aquatic pen. The wire seemed to protect him from angry beavers, but I knew the pen wouldn't stop a determined bear.

I added a floating platform in the pen and on this I put an old plastic pet carrier. I covered the carrier with branches, sedges, and chunks of turf, building a mini beaver lodge. This also gave him a spot to crawl out of the water, where he could dry off, groom, and sleep in the warmth of the sun. When he went inside, the lodge offered his eyes protection from the same bright light. Beavers have presumably evolved to prefer being active during dusk and dawn, and most seek some protection from direct sunlight.

To add a touch of diversity to the quickly disappearing vegetation within the pen, I would pick floating pads from the large water lilies on a nearby lake and float them in his pen. At around three months of age, he had finally learned to dive and would submerge under the water on one side of the pen and pop up under a large pad, wearing it on his head like a slimy helmet, from under which he would peer around suspiciously. He reminded me of Arte Johnson of *Laugh-In* fame and I half-expected him to say, "Veddy inta-resting!" When he felt all was well, he would slip quietly back, allowing the pad to settle, unruffled, on the water. When he got tired or bored of this game, he ate the lily pads, holding them like tortillas.

With that one exception after Mike's funeral, I wondered at Cameron's overall indifference to affection and inability to bond, either with me or with his siblings. Not that it's necessarily wise for a wild animal to show affection to humans. As a matter of fact it's usually a bad thing, and I take great measures to prevent human familiarity with most of my wards. The previous young beaver I raised, Eh, had showered his sibling Bea as well as me with grooming, attention, and murmurs of comfort, and he still ended up being a normal, well-adapted beaver. I wondered if Cameron were perhaps emotionally challenged, beaver-wise. Not a good thing, considering the close bonds beaver family units form, enabling them to work together effectively for their mutual survival.

# Laughter Is the Best Medicine

The unusually warm fall made rearing Cameron just a little bit easier, and since I was still feeling quite depressed, I welcomed anything that lightened my workload. I was able to let Cameron exercise outside well into November, and he even had an occasional outdoor swim in December. Normally, the pond would have had a thick covering of ice by mid-November. Unlike the time I had overwintered Eh, our new house had running water and sewer connections in the basement. But I was kind of proud of my new rehab room with its shiny, clean white walls, computers, and filing cabinets. I didn't want to witness what Cameron's inquisitive teeth would do to the decor, or see his soiled bath water spackling my newly painted walls

There was always Bruce's nice two-car garage! Cameron had already spent summer nights and stormy days in the cardboard carton set up for him there. After all, Bruce had taken a temporary job placement in Sault Ste. Marie and wasn't always home to witness to what the little dickens destroyed when he was free in the garage. I knew he would let me fix up a home there for Cameron, if only to help cheer me up. Since he hadn't put up a fuss about Eh when he stayed in the basement of our first house, Cameron's taking up space in the garage would be much more acceptable. I would still need to haul water for his bath, but at least I wouldn't be hauling it up and down stairs like before. Plus, the garage was insulated and could be heated if necessary. As all beavers can, Cameron could tolerate very cool and even very cold temperatures, so I wasn't too concerned about providing supplementary heating.

I set about building a four-foot-by-eight-foot enclosure in one of the two parking spaces to replace the temporary cardboard carton.

"Just using my side of the garage, Bruce, honest!" I cajoled, when he came to inspect my handiwork. "I don't need to put my truck in the garage this winter. It's supposed to be a mild one."

The short pressboard walls, framed with two-by-fours, were set up over several layers of heavy-duty plastic sheeting. Layers of newspaper covered the plastic to provide insulation and to soak up spills and waste material. The layers of paper would be changed regularly. It was an easy task to dispose of it, since once it was wet, Cameron himself would bunch it up and push it into a corner. Several inches of dry, clean straw were scattered on top of the layers of newspaper. A large cardboard carton with a hole cut in its side and stuffed with straw was his lodge. The cardboard lodge took a lot of abuse and needed to be replaced at least once a week. The straw-lined box kept him cozy and warm, even when the temperature in the garage dropped below freezing.

A saying I used to hear as a kid went something like, "For Satan finds some mischief still/For idle hands to do." I always figured this was just a line my elders made up to ensure I did my chores. Its foreboding tone worked well to keep me busy as a child. I discovered it was also a good philosophy to apply to Cameron's busy beaver fingers.

I tried to keep him occupied with little tasks. Chores that I left for him to do included disposing of the large armfuls of tiny little sticks, saplings and tree bark that I deposited in a pile for him to carry and rearrange, one by one, on top of or inside his lodge. I carried in pails of mud for him to empty and smear around. I filled another corner of his pen with blocks of fresh straw for him to push, snuffle, and chew on. The more tasks he had to do, the fewer times I had to mend the gnawed hole that kept showing up in the corner of the walled enclosure. The 17th-century English minister Isaac Watts was right: as long as Cameron's little hands weren't idle, he wasn't getting into mischief. Best of all, my keeping busy keeping Cameron busy, helped my state of mind, too! It was all very therapeutic.

I was glad I was able to house Cameron within the sturdy walls of the garage, since the bears were coming through the yard regularly even into November. They would have been sticking close to their winter dens, so I deduced their sleeping spots were nearby. We had been lucky and hadn't had any major nuisance bear problems around the pens or yard, so far. However, I was worried that the odour from the boxes of distressed vegetables and fruit stored in the garage might be enough to tempt a bear to break in, and I was further worried that once in, a bear might eat Cameron. One day, when I returned home and heard a tremendous thumping coming from the garage, I feared my concerns had become reality. I cautiously opened the door and peered in.

My senses were overwhelmed by the smell as I pushed the door open. The acrid, medicinal smell of overripe, moldy oranges burned my eyes and nose. And there was that strange thumping noise again! As my eyes adapted to the gloom, I saw the overturned, empty waxed boxes, which not long ago had been brimming with overripe fruit and vegetables, destined for the rabbits. A wide, slimy smear dotted with the occasional blob of colour crossed the cement floor from the boxes to Cameron's enclosure. Brooms, shovels, and scraps of lumber leaned askew against Cameron's enclosure as well. How odd!

A quick glance at the intact window screens assured me no bear had broken in. A poor old sickly hen I had isolated for treatment had been pushed, pet carrier and all, against Cameron's pen. The carrier wobbled as the poor old bird beat her wings and struggled for footing on the floor of her precariously angled crate, accounting for the thumping sounds I had heard. The mouse pens, once neatly stacked in the back part of the garage, had also been pushed, but fortunately not opened, against the pile of tools and boards. Dozens of black, beady eyes peered out from behind the fruit-smeared glass, while frantic mother mice raced back and forth carrying pink babies in their mouths and trying desperately to pull together their tumbled nests.

The fruit- and veggie-juice smear led to the escape hole in the corner of Cameron's pen, which had once again been gnawed open. Green remnants of overripe romaine lettuce hung in stringy globs from the rough slivers on the side of the gnawed hole. Throughout the pen and in various corners, several hundred pieces of fruit and vegetables were piled neatly and not-so-neatly, some squashed, some whole, varying in size from grapes to heads of lettuce. His cardboard lodge, now pushed to the centre of the pen, was brimming, bulging, and smeared with juices, with a broomstick sticking out the top like a banner from a medieval turret.

In the past, Cameron had routinely concealed his escape hole with straw or soiled newspaper after having returned from an adventure outside. This time, the hole had been sealed with a large bag of distressed buns and bread, intended for rabbit treats.

For the first time in what seemed like ages, I found myself fighting to control a snicker. Then as the enormity of his antics struck me, I started an uncontrolled belly laugh that shook me from head to foot. As I snorted and honked, weak with laughter, I felt the darkness and sadness of the past few months lift from me like a huge weight. Despite the sticky mess I would need to deal with, this was the most therapeutic thing that could have happened. I continued to shake with laughter as tears ran down my cheeks. Curious as to what the ruckus was all about, Cameron squeezed out of his soggy cardboard box, still gripping some juicy piece of fruit. I reached down and lifted him from the goopy mess that surrounded him. But before I could set him down on the somewhat cleaner floor of the garage, he whined and rubbed his sticky face on my hair and cheek, peach slobbers dripping down my tear-streaked face.

It took me the remainder of the day to clean up the mess Cameron had created in a few short hours. Mind you, he hadn't had a cranky, sticky, furry thing slapping and pinch-biting the back of his legs and hindering his work, as I did. His cardboard sleeping box was gooey, fragrant, and soaked with juices. Boards and tools that he had somehow managed to wedge into the enclosure stretched and warped the sides of the box into a rhomboid shape. Puddles of fruit and vegetable juices formed a kaleidoscope of colours on the plastic lining of the floor.

I made a mental note to pick up a replacement cardboard box from the local furniture store when I was in town the next day. But he was darned well going to have to sleep in the sticky mess overnight, and it served him right. I did, however, mop up the juices and pulp from the floor to prevent stains on the cement beneath, and to keep him from smearing it around even more. As I left the garage, looking forward to a hot shower to clean the vegetable and fruit cocktails out of my hair, I heard his nummy-nummy-nummying as he nibbled on the juice-soaked cardboard box. I felt light-headed and slightly euphoric, perhaps from inhaling the fragrance of so much fermented fruit, but more likely because a few moments' mirth and merriment had eased a sadness I had felt for far too long.

Overindulgence of fruits and vegetables can cause terrible stomach problems in animals, and Cameron desperately needed some tender loving care the next day. His little tummy roared, gurgled, and erupted violently.

Oh, great! More cleanups to deal with, I thought. I figured I'd better get a second box in case he sullied the new one right away with his defecations.

Fortunately, Pepto-Bismol along with a goodly gnaw on ginger root, was enough to soothe his digestive problems.

I would never have believed how much laughter could heal the soul. I found I was no longer plodding through my chores from day to day. I realized just how much I had been missing or overlooking during my blue funk.

For example, I should have noticed how Cameron had grown in the past few weeks. This became glaringly apparent when I replaced his sodden box. As usual, I used an ice-cream pail lid as a template to mark the size of the entrance hole I needed to cut out for him. Having done so, I put the box back in place and filled it with clean straw. I saw him struggle a bit to get through the hole I had just cut out, thinking it was the straw blocking him. But when I watched him stick his head out, his front legs scrabbling and dragging the box behind him, I realized I needed to increase the size of the hole. With his stick-and-mud-covered abode stuck on his back, Cameron looked like an oversized caddisfly larva dragging a gigantic stick-adorned casing. He wheezed angrily at my laughter when I climbed in to free him.

Life was more or less uneventful for the rest of the fall and into winter. The weather stayed relatively mild and Cameron seemed happy to sleep and play within the confines of his garage enclosure. There were a few attempted escapes, most likely when an innate urge to collect food overwhelmed him. Although none of them mirrored the magnificent results of his fruit adventure, Cameron did have at least one other dose of excitement. During one escape, a pelican temporarily sharing his garage chased him around, snapping his bill loudly but harmlessly over the bewildered beaver. I walked in to the fray in time to see Cameron struggling to get back into his box as the pelican kept clapping his bill over his ample backside. I really think the silly bird thought he could swallow him.

After that unnerving incident, Cameron would jump fearfully at any loud clap, which I have to think is not a particularly good twitch for an animal that relies on loud tail slaps for communication.

# Love Heals, Too!

One day in February, Cameron developed a cough. When I used an ear thermometer on him (maybe not the best method, considering the beaver's tiny ears, but certainly the least invasive), it indicated he might be running a fever. As the day went on, he seemed to worsen. He became lethargic and turned off his food. When I climbed into the enclosure with him, he perked up significantly, cuddling up to me and whining. I don't like to give antibiotics to my wards except in the most dire of cases. Antibiotics had not saved Hunny, so I prayed that this time, if I had to use them, they would do their magic. I needed his weight, however, to give to my vet so Cameron could be prescribed an accurate dosage. I hadn't lifted him lately, and he resisted when I tried to pick him up. When he had been younger, I could get him to climb into his little basket, which made it easy to weigh him. I tried that now. I zeroed the bathroom scales to my weight and balanced on them myself, while trying to convince Cameron to climb into the basket I held. No way!

Now, beavers can be amorous little fellows, and I guess February is a lonely month without company. Seeing me standing there in the low light of the garage in my puffy, brown insulated coveralls and shiny black boots, it seems he didn't see me as his foster mom, he saw a potential girlfriend. Embarrassing as his amorous attentions to my leg were, they served my purpose well. He had grabbed me around my knee with a determined grip, and climbed onto my boot. His loving embrace was so tenacious I was able to stand on one leg, and with Cameron firmly attached, lift the other in the air. While holding him up like this, I tried to read the scale. We bounced, thirty-five pounds, forty-five, thirty-five, forty-five, forty, forty. With a contented sigh, he climbed down and was back to his normal self. Me, I went back to the house, carrying my sullied coveralls straight to the laundry room. En route, I promised myself that my next purchase would be a platform scale, and that I would speak of this humiliating encounter to no one.

I determined that Cameron did not need antibiotics that night, but he did get a large stuffed toy beaver for company. He immediately focused on its face, grooming and gripping the fake fur in his hands, murmuring softly. I had been replaced in his heart with polyester fibrefill and button eyes. By the next day, the cough had disappeared, so I guess it's true, love heals all. He spent the following weeks cuddling his new sweetheart, even dragging it into the tub with him. My attempt to take it from him so I could wash it was met with a level of beaver attitude I hadn't seen from him before: he hissed and puffed and lunged at me, grinding his incisors. I left him to groom his sodden mate and went about my work.

The pond opened up early that spring. Normally there is ice on it well into May, but we were pleasantly surprised by the unseasonably warm weather. By April, although Cameron was not even a year old, I thought his body size should give him the confidence he needed to fend for himself in the pond. I figured I could slowly reintroduce him to the resident beavers. Initially, I put him in the large dog pen the Stewardship rangers and I had built for him the past summer. The enclosure was still set up near the pond, but as the water level had dropped over the winter and the pond levels hadn't yet reached the previous year's depth, the pen was now on dry land. This meant I had to provide a large plastic kiddy pool full of water for him. Now, though, he was very strong and determined to be free. He rocked his pool back and forth with his temper tantrums, slopping out the water as soon as I filled it. Then he gnawed holes in the plastic, searching for the soft mud that he felt should have been lining the bottom. As he focused his attentions on digging a hole under the

Brownie seemed to be totally at ease around the beaver pond.

Brownie and Eh having one of many standoffs. Mud would soon fly.

Lucky, Janice, Eh, and Brownie would utter soft calls to each other when they met like this.

Brownie stomps on poor little wood frogs.

Brownie's hair stood on end just before lightning struck nearby.

Brownie would chew on tree trunks and branches when he was cutting his teeth.

Over the course of a winter, Lil often ends up with several great grey owls.

Lil was able to provide Janice with her basic needs, but what she really needed was companionship.

A logger, who had inadvertently cut their nest tree, drove a long distance to deliver these young great grey owls to Lil.

When threatened, American pelicans put up a lot of huff and bluff, with loud clapping of their bills and false charges and lunges.

This young merlin is basking in the sun. Sunlight helps feathers develop and stimulates preening.

A young mallard knows instinctively what to eat, but relies on mom for warmth, protection, and guidance.

Cameron with some of his offspring.

Cameron and Hunny enthusiastically enjoying their bottles.

Cameron, Lucky, and Janice in a moment of truce, sharing food at the pond's edge.

Cutting and chipping, clipping and hauling, Cameron slowly created clearings within the once-dense aspen stands.

Foxes often behave more like cats than dogs.

Another of Lil's adorable wards.

P'silla enjoying one of her treats.

One of P'silla's first big achievements was developing the ability to debark branches.

P'silla played for hours by herself on the brick patio, spending time exploring bags of peat moss and plant pots.

Persephone would stare Cameron down with her back arched, tail up, and hoof mid-air, as the beaver hissed and puffed.

Off Persephone flew, snorting and blowing.

Persephone trotting along the shoreline of the pond.

pen, I realized I was going to have to release him to the pond sooner than I had planned.

"Okay, Cammy, you're on your own! I can't protect you any more." I had known this day would come, but I worried whether he were really ready. He was such a softy, and he wasn't even a year old. Young beavers usually aren't forced to fend for themselves until they reach two years of age.

I opened the door of the kennel, and out he waddled. He wheezed at me a few times, turned to the pond's edge and swam directly out into the main channel. I may not have mentioned how much weight he had gained over the winter. Cameron should have weighed twenty-five pounds or thereabouts. His tail, utilized to store fat, should have been about four inches wide and half an inch thick, but was instead six inches wide and one and a quarter inches thick. He was thirty-six inches from the tip of his nose to the base of his tail. His weight now? Fifty-five pounds!

Since the love-in weigh-in in February, I had gained a new, more accurate method of weighing him According to my new scales he had gained an additional fifteen pounds! Wild beavers would be steadily losing weight during the dead of the winter, but not so Cammy! He kept packing on the pounds! This size would give him a definite physical and psychological edge if it came to duking it out with his reluctant hosts.

A resident male was first to swim to mid-pond and check him out. After a few minutes of wheezing, a small altercation took place, with Cameron the instigator, but Cameron didn't appear to damage anything more than some beaver ego. Then a female beaver, even larger than Cameron, put the run on him, their v-shaped ripples carving up the pond's smooth surface. Cameron paddled his bulk for all he was worth, trying to avoid her wrath, but his pampered garage life had left him out of shape. I realized I had to let the beavers settle their differences without my interference if Cameron were to find his place in the pond with them. I reluctantly left the pond edge while the female was pursuing Cameron and the gap between them was closing quickly. I didn't want to watch anymore, in case I decided to call him back to safety. His release lifted a major nightly chore from my shoulders. I used the first evening of his release to put my feet up and observe. From my high balcony, drink in one hand, Enya playing softly in the background, I watched the wild beavers and Cammy interact, one moment all appearing friendly, sniffing at each other, the next having hissy fits and slapping and pushing each

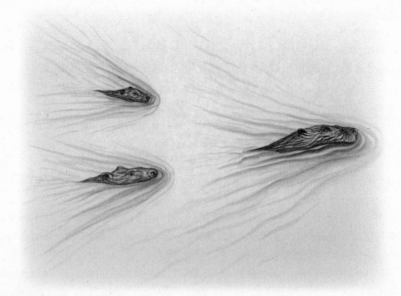

other around. Mosquitoes and darkness eventually drove me inside, but when I listened through the patio screens, I could hear squealing and whining. This continued into the evening and far into the night.

The next morning when I went to check on Cameron, I realized the confrontations must have gone on all night. The entire pond was churned up. Dark, muddy trails snaked through the silvery dew on the grass, evidence the beavers had taken their discussions to terra firma. Now, as the sun rose, they were all congregated mid-pond. While the other beavers dived and attacked from below, Cameron just bobbed and floated. I realized he was now too fat to dive. While the other beavers swam around with only their heads out of water, Cameron's entire back and backside floated high, a good two or three inches above the surface. They came at him from below the waterline, trying to nip him.

Each time they hit him, it reminded me of what it's like to try to grab a beach ball from under water. Like the ball, he would just pop up higher. When the pond beavers tried to hold Cameron's head under water, they couldn't, because he was too buoyant. Instead, they rolled off his back in disgust. But when the scene of them poking and bouncing Cameron began to resemble a television documentary I once watched of killer whales playing catch with baby seals, I stepped in.

From the edge of the pond where Cameron could see me, I stood and called his name. Beavers may be fearless when fighting one of their own, but the older ones were not about to take on this loud, two-legged entity to which the chubby one swam. Still, Cameron was not about to be bullied, as he loved his freedom too much. He only came to me for a brief corner talk and a few slices of bread. I felt I should be holding his mouthguard and a towel. With a quick nose-bump goodbye, he gamely swam back amongst the five resident beavers—the adult male, the female and three of last year's kits—which were now lined up in a row at what they must have felt was a safe distance from me.

I gave up on the idea of trying to rescue him and left the six of them to determine their pecking order. It was obvious that defending himself came natural to Cameron—maybe all that pent-up anger after being the victim of his siblings' ear-sucking could now be vented. And so far he had fared well; I could see no blood or missing parts on him. On the other hand, the other beavers also seemed none the worse for wear.

After a few days and nights of loud vocalization and frantic splashing, things seemed more civil. Cameron appeared to be fixated on the big female and followed her everywhere, whining as he swam. All previous affections to stuffed toys and baggy coveralls were obviously forgotten. The little adult male, much smaller than Cameron, tried to ward off Cameron's advances towards his mate. But Cameron would just swim over top of him like a tank, or, more accurately, a low-flying dirigible.

It seemed the only time there was peace on the pond was during bright, hot sunny days. On these halcyon days, the resident beavers would retire to their house, the newer of two lodges on the pond. To enter the house, they had to dive deep and travel down carved-out runways, which formed the entrance of their lodge. That left Cameron outside, unable to join his new love in her chambers since, try as he might, he could not swim below the surface of the water. Aside from his own buoyancy, part of his diving problem may have been inexperience. In his leaner days he'd never had the opportunity, or the need. My artificial ponds had been only about sixteen inches deep. When I'd offered him the opportunity as a kit to swim in the deeper waters of the pond under my supervision, he never seemed to want to dive deep.

He was forced to live in Eh's old house, which in its current state of disrepair and low water had several large openings in the side. These entrances would have been submerged in days of higher water, but when Eh and his extended family had outgrown the original machine-excavated pond, they had built a new dam downstream and created a new, larger pool by flooding what had been a sedge meadow. They also stopped doing repairs on the first dam, which contained the original pond, and as a result the water in the man-made pond subsided. The end result, though, was a much larger body of water.

At least Cameron could use the exposed entrances to walk into the protection of the decrepit lodge. I would watch as he disappeared into the darkness, always mumbling to himself as he went. He habitually dragged along a freshly clipped piece of foliage to nibble on, which helped him pass the time until his lady came out to play again.

The initial melt of snow in the bush and fields had occurred quickly that spring, filling the newer ponds to their brims, before slowly spilling over a series of three dams, eventually passing through a road culvert below. The fact that the water in the old pond was relatively low had been a blessing, and by holding back the main force of the spring freshet, prevented the torrents of runoff from wiping out the roadbed. Road crews had not thawed the ice out of the large culvert, which ran under the road downstream of the pond, so the water, once it reached the culvert, had nowhere to flow. Instead, some ran down the ditch to the downstream bog and some eroded the soft sand at the sides of the culvert. Both actions were compromising the roadbed and would spell trouble, if further rains should come.

And they did. Normally, I could open a trough in the dam and keep it free of debris long enough to drop the pond to my preferred level which, incidentally, was not the same level desired by the beavers. But until the road crews opened the frozen culvert and repaired the undermined road in the vicinity of the bog, they had advised me not to break the dam for fear of washing out the road.

Despite this warning, I was not about to let the beavers turn my entire yard into a flooded meadow, no matter how happy it would make them. For weeks, I would go morning and night and release the waters from above the dam at a rate I figured the still largely iced-up road culvert could handle.

Cameron seemed to think this was great fun. He would swim back and forth in the swirling, turbid waters of the small waterfalls I created when I broke the dam, letting the currents carry him right to the edge of the dam before he'd make an effort to swim back out. It must have been a hoot, for he did it over and over and over. But when he finally tired of the game, his beaver senses took over and he knew instinctively that flowing water is not a good thing. Then I would have to choke back laughter, for he would climb into the newly opened trough, face the rushing water, and then push at it with his paws. This would cause the plume of water to hit his chest, rush up under his chin and flow over his head like a rooster's tail. Meanwhile, his chubby body would completely plug the trough, until the force of the water caused him to lose his footing and he would be swept down to the next pond. Undaunted, he would rush back up the slope of the dam and start anew.

As I hacked and dug at the mud and sticks, tossing them out of the trough, he brought in more, poking and jabbing large, sharply pointed beaver chews in my direction. This was done with such gusto that I was often left with large bruises and scratches. Once, while I focused on cleaning away debris the beavers had added the previous night, I was none-too-gently pushed aside with a large log, destined for the largest opening in the dam. As his large brown form squeezed past in the wake of this battering ram, the beaver hissed angrily at me.

Cameron is certainly acting rude today, I thought, as I continued my task.

Then, a similar bump on my other side, followed with an apologetic wheeze, made me stop cold in my boots. There were two large beavers in the trough, one on each side of my legs, which meant one of them was not my gentle friend!

Beavers, when cornered, threatened, or even just ticked off, may take a run at the offending party, which in this case was me. I figured now was a good time to back away from my morning's labour, and let Cameron and his lady friend fix the damage I had done to their edifice. Anything else might be bad judgment.

The beavers remained a great source of entertainment for me that spring. When I took my sojourn on the balcony in the evening to do my Backyard Frog Survey, I relaxed on my lounge chair, watching the antics of the beavers until the last ray of light gilded the pond. The inevitable drone of mosquitoes rising from the mud would eventually drive me into the house. As spring wore on, beavers began to appear in the twilight en masse.

In the early part of the spring, there had been at least five pond beavers, plus Cameron, inhabiting the pond, but those numbers mysteriously grew to thirteen! Their shapes could be mistaken for brown lumps of mud, unless the rippling water around the lump gave away its true identity, as they chewed and uprooted sedges. They were very efficient at turning the meadow into a pond. As the water levels rose, the sedge meadow became soaked and the hardpan clays softened, and then the beavers started to excavate runways, accessing new areas of grasses and sedge. The beavers would dig up and consume these plants—tussocks, roots, and all. The softened, disturbed soil would then be hauled to the dam, enabling the beavers to raise the water even further. Canals were carved into the soft mud and clay, which gave the beavers deeper and therefore safer cover in the water. I watched as my pond frontage grew and grew.

Well, I thought as I peered out one morning at the new flood plain, at least Bruce won't have to burn or mow as much of the meadow anymore to keep down the tick population.

Eventually, the city repaired the roads and I was able to bring the pond to a level we all seemed to agree with. The beavers and I had a respite from the daily dam-breaking/dam-building activities, once the pond reached a stable and tolerable level.

The enlarged pond was by then big enough to attract more species of shorebirds and waterfowl. They fed in the pond, some courted and a few felt safe to stay and breed there. Even a strange-looking, shy sora rail raised a family of coal-black chicks, which were hatched in a small sedge-lined nest, precariously balanced above the rising waters. Muskrat, mink, and otter joined the community. Now when I saw the brown lumps and ripples along the edge, I had to use binoculars to determine who was who.

There was no mistaking Cameron! The only things he could possibly have been mistaken for would be a small moose or bear. Compared to the other beavers he was huge, his size amplified by the fact he was still so buoyant, floating high in the water, his ripples pushing across the mudflats like a tsunami. On more than one occasion I watched him munching away on sedges, only to see a red-winged blackbird strut across his tail to pick up a drowning dragonfly from the water, or a swamp sparrow scratching at seeds that had fallen from the sedges onto his furry back. Cameron didn't seem to mind these feathered hitchhikers much, until a fat drake mallard climbed up on Cameron's ample backside to preen. Pushed to his limit of friendly tolerance, Cameron slapped and thrashed and hissed and chased the mallard all the way across the pond.

It was during this added spring activity when the youngest of the pond beavers left to find territories of their own. Shortly after, the dejected adult male, who had obviously been bested by Cameron, continued the exodus. I think I first became aware of their absence when the pond began to seem noticeably calmer at night. There were now just the two beavers, and Cameron seemed smug when he came to me for his nightly treat of yams, his lady at his side.

Now that he was the male of the lodge, Cameron became very protective of the pond. Geese, ducks, and muskrats voiced their annoyance at his possessive displays, shuffling out of his way but wise enough to avoid his tantrums. All this added activity helped strengthen him, and even though he still floated high when he swam, he had overcome his handicap and had learned to dive deeply. He was now able to disappear under the water, popping up beside intruders such as ducks, sending them shrieking off the pond.

With such abundant activity in and around the pond, it became a photographer's dream. Bruce was eager to take full advantage of wonderful opportunities such as closeups of pairs of waterfowl, brilliant in mating plumage, so he built a blind near the shore. One evening, as he set up to photograph what were now ongoing courtship displays, I remained out of sight on the hill, not wanting to frighten away his subjects. When I sat on the slope during one of my many breaks to watch the scene on the pond below, I was thrilled at the flurry of activity. Teals and mallards twirled and dabbled in front of the blind and since I had last looked four large Canada geese were making their way slowly to the pile of grain along the shore. A large wave forming near the shore indicated Cameron had come to investigate, too.

From my view on the hill, I chuckled. I could see two wiggling posteriors sticking out through the back of the blind. One rump was covered in camouflage hunting pants; the second, much shorter, was covered with hair with a large, flat tail attached. When I changed my angle on the scene, I could see Cameron peering out through a hole in the lower portion of the blind. Bruce, oblivious to his blind-mate, continued to focus on his subjects. Cameron finally gave up in disgust when he realized Bruce had no goodies for him. After scent-marking Bruce's camera bag, he slipped back into the water and proceeded to chase off the feeding geese. I chuckled at his audacity and although I would love to have watched longer, I started to push myself up off the grass to return to work.

I froze at a familiar "huu-onk" beside me. While I had been intent on watching the amusing scene below, two geese had left the water and made their way up the hill to where I sat. One hesitated to come any closer and stopped to feed on the lush grass on the septic field, while the other approached me with her neck stretched out. When I whispered, "Janice?" she "wee-wee-ed" happily and laid her head across my lap.

She looked great! There was no residual droop in her wings from her early nutritional problems and her new adult feathers were shiny and healthy. I assumed that the more cautious goose may have been Lucky, or perhaps Lucky was one of the remaining two geese still feeding by the pond, and this was Janice's new mate. It would make sense that these geese were familiar with my pond and its permanent residents. Earlier, when Cameron had tried his bullying bluffs to drive them off the pond, they had ignored him instead of fleeing. Those new to Cameron's tactics would almost always flee.

The geese hung around the pond for a week or more, making me hope that they would nest there, as yearlings sometimes nest if suitable territories are available. They definitely went through mating rituals on the pond. But perhaps it was just too small, or the family of mink and otter that regularly cruised through spooked them, because after a while, they left.

Later that summer I saw two geese with a single gosling on the pond. They spent the day feeding and preening. Tracks in the dry dust along the road revealed they had walked some distance from a small lake to get to our beaver pond. If one of the pair was Janice or Lucky, they were wild enough now to keep the gosling far from me, a very good sign, but familiar enough to come searching for a handout near the feeding station. I was pleased.

Rehabbers dream of being able to follow up on the outcome of their wards, but are not often so lucky. I realized imprinting and conditioning can be reversible in young animals, provided they are given the opportunity to go back to the wild. It also meant that cases I had in the past dismissed as hopeless might not have been, if they had been allowed the same opportunities as Lucky and Janice. Not something I wanted to dwell on, but definitely a lesson for the future.

# A Prickly Situation

One day after finishing my chores earlier than expected, I took advantage of my free time to work on a magazine article I was writing. I was on a roll, and the words were flowing easily. Great, I thought, no writer's block today.

As I rattled away at the keyboard, sounds from outside drew my thoughts away my work. Over the crow of the rooster, the erratic explosions of pigeon wings, and the unrestrained laughter from the resident mallards, I heard a sweet, soft call, summoning me, or more specifically, summoning more food.

"Hink, hink, hink...." More demanding now: "*Hink hink hink*, doot doot doot...." No longer so soft, but still appealing. "*Do-it, do-it, do-it.*" At that last outcry, I sighed, filed my latest changes and shut down the computer. So much for keeping my creative juices flowing.

P'silla wants food, so P'silla gets food.

Shortly after Cameron gained his freedom, I had enjoyed a brief furlough. In this occupation, though, respites are usually brief. A small porcupette joined my facilities that spring and once again I became willingly indentured to the demands of a little critter.

P'silla the porcupine came to me in early spring, a result of what seems to be a common and constantly growing cause for orphaned wildlife—that is, the intolerance of human beings.

It had become a pattern. Each day, after tending to patients already in my care, I would reply to an ever-growing number of phone messages on my answering machine. Some calls were easy to deal with, and only required a bit of advice regarding wildlife behaviour. Others were more urgent, and not easily resolved. Such was the case regarding a young porcupine. The lady who answered my return call sounded both disgusted and concerned.

"My neighbour shot a porcupine a few days ago, and now there is a baby wandering around crying," she said, "I don't know why he shot it, she's been around here for years and didn't do any harm."

My hope was that the baby might not have to be taken in for care, as porcupettes are independent early in life, at least with respect to self-feeding, and nature has provided them the benefits of a spiny protection when mom isn't around.

"How big is it?" I hoped the response would describe a porcupine a foot or more in length. Then my job would be easy. All I would need to do is have it relocated to a safer spot.

"Oh, maybe eight inches, tops, from nose to tip of tail," she said.

Darn! It would need help. When she asked if she should look around for possible siblings, I assured her that porcupettes are only children. Twins are rare, if not unheard-of.

I often need to depend on the callers to pick up and deliver to me the waifs they find, but only if I can be sure they and the patient are safe from further injury. Even babies can hurt their rescuers when they are scared. In order for me to find time to work an eight-hour regular job, tend to my patients, and deal with life's other demands, I count on the kindness of those who can deliver new patients to me safely. Fortunately, the caller's neighbour and his daughter were willing to capture the little porcupette and deliver it to a prearranged meeting point. I suggested ways to protect themselves and the baby from injury, and set out to meet them. After introductions and exchanging information regarding the circumstances of the mother's demise, we walked to the back of their vehicle. There, huddled in a corner of a Styrofoam cooler, was a teensy-weensy porcupine. I knew then the right decision was to take it in for care … it was much too young to survive for long on its own. I carefully

loaded it into the wood-shaving-lined box I had brought with me, and after thanking the porcupette's rescuers headed home.

For many years porcupines were virtually absent from our area. Even today, their numbers remain very low in northwestern Ontario. I had no experience therefore with porcupines young or old, having only observed a few from a distance and never having even seen a baby, let alone raised one. My past experience was limited to commanding a timely "*No! Off!*" to my dogs when we encountered the big fellow who was living on our pine ridge, before they received the inevitable face full of quills. Fortunately, good training and maybe a bit of common sense had so far prevented Heidi and Brill from contact.

I had witnessed the ability of porcupine quills to penetrate almost any material, from the thick lips and tongue of my brother's old husky, to the heavy, vulcanized rubber of tires and safety boots. In fact, one of my brothers, while cutting pulpwood one winter, hadn't seen a porcupine in the branches of a thick spruce until it fell out of the tree and landed on his foot. It managed a quick tail swipe before plodding off through the snow, leaving several shiny ebony and ivory reminders in his steel-toed safety boots. Another brother was once compelled to assist a tiny porcupine that was struggling to climb out of a ditch, by gently lifting it out of the trench with the toe of his boot. He too, was left with a souvenir of tiny, perfect quills from his passive interaction.

Once, while driving home after work, I couldn't avoid running over the lifeless body of a large female porcupine that had paid the price for seeking the pleasures of road salt in the centre. I stopped to remove her body to a more dignified resting place and searched the immediate vicinity for a possible orphan. Female mammals of a number of species seek road salt to aid milk production, and despite her swollen mammary glands, which indicated she was nursing, I didn't find her youngster. I stooped along the roadside to collect the scattered quills for a friend who I knew would welcome such treasures for her First Nations cultural art. It was then I noticed quills stuck into the tread and sidewalls of my tire. Despite my efforts to remove them, they stayed embedded, and remained so for several weeks.

I have the utmost respect for the spiny armour worn by porcupines and knew I would have to take special precautions and care with this little one. Out came my collection of *Wildlife Rehabilitation Today* journals, and I skimmed the index searching for information on porcupines. I finally came across a short article. Not much to go on, but at least it was a start. I figured raising a porcupine would be similar to raising a beaver, just drier and pricklier.

The article I referred to described a recommended feeding formula, and suggested wrapping the porcupette in a thick towel when handling, while taking the normal precautions to prevent it from inhaling formula.

Great, I can do this, I thought.

I wrapped the tiny female in a thick, heavy towel and proceeded to feed her a warmed goat's-milk-based orphan mammal formula diluted with electrolytes. She wasn't exhibiting any signs of dehydration, so I didn't think it was necessary to start her on the straight electrolytes that some young foundlings require. She ate readily and hungrily, whimpering and "dooting" the whole time. Her soft lisp made me think of a prissy little girl, gentle and quiet. When I wrote up her record that evening, I hesitated, then scrawled "P'silla" in the narrow column by her statistics, no room for the full "Prisilla." The lisping little sounds she made were so endearing, I had to reflect them in her name.

After she drank her fill, she struggled to get down off my lap. I gently started to unwind her from the towel so I could set her on the floor. I discovered that whoever had suggested they be wrapped in towel was sadly mistaken, or had used a very special towel, indeed. Her tiny quills stuck her tighter to the towel than a butterscotch candy to a chenille bedspread. Her twisting, turning, squirming, and "dooting," as she struggled added to both our distress levels. I slipped off my leather gloves to give me more dexterity in freeing her from the towel.

That was another big mistake! Brushing the exposed quills, I received a set into my wrist, barely missing a large, pulsing vein. That made me queasy! I hoped that it didn't hurt her to lose her quills as much as it hurt me to remove them from my flesh. After the tears of pain subsided, I examined the tiny weapons carefully to see what I was dealing with.

Each quill was soft at the base, and just like the newly developing feathers of a bird, the soft part was full of blood. The business end had razor-sharp barbs. Fortunately, porcupine quills are believed to contain a natural antibiotic, and the punctures would not likely become infected. I wrapped my wounds quickly, and set back to the task of freeing P'silla from her cocoon. I tried several methods to unwrap her as she squealed and struggled, and wrapped herself tighter into the terry cloth. I had no choice … I had to try the Band-Aid removal method.

"This is gonna hurt, little one, but it's for the best," I said unconvincingly.

Pulling the towel swiftly in the direction of the quills' growth brought only a little squeal, and a lot of tiny, armed spears.

I'm not sure who was more shaken by this awful experience, but there would certainly be no repeats. The porcupette would be drinking her formula from a dish from now on. And any necessary handling for weighing or medical examinations would be on her terms. We developed a mutually agreeable method of transport. I would wear leather gauntlets made for handling the big birds of prey, allowing her to climb onto my outstretched hand. Carrying her that way was safe and comfortable for both of us. Best of all, she quickly forgot or forgave me for that first nasty piece of business I put her through.

She seemed to really like the smell and taste of the heavy leather gauntlets, perhaps because they retained traces of salts used in the tanning process, or perhaps from my perspiration. She'd focus her attention on them and took every opportunity to chew them. Fortunately, she still had the tiny, white milk teeth of a baby rodent and couldn't damage the leather. Her fixation on the gloves allowed me to use them as a babysitting device. If for some reason I had to leave her on her own when she exercised in the yard, I would lay the gloves down in a safe, shady spot. She would happily waddle over and sit on them, sucking on the thumbs and snuffling her head up the cuffs, until I returned to gather her up. I learned quickly to check for spiny little gifts left behind in the wristbands before putting them on. These passive guardians worked fine for several days. But then one day after leaving her with the gloves to tend to an errand, I returned to where I had left her—and only one glove remained to mark the spot.

I remembered that whenever she was wrestling the gloves or doing battle with a bush, she would vocalize. Sure enough, as I listened carefully, somewhere out in the distance came a soft "hink hink hink." I scanned the sedges in the meadow and noticed there was a clump swaying suspiciously.

When I went to investigate, there was P'silla, a finger of the glove firmly gripped in her teeth, struggling to pull it through a sedge tussock. Who knows where she was intending to take it, but I put a stop to her plans. Following some push and pull and loud discussion, I won. After removing a few tiny quills, I cautiously slipped the sodden glove onto my hand. Despite her erected quill displays, and her pinch-biting on my leg, I left her on the ground. She would have to learn how to find her own way home, and best for her to do it while I was there to supervise. I headed back to the house away from the hordes of mosquitoes and soggy ground, watching her out of the corner of my eye.

Her sad little "doot doot doots" grew distant behind me. I turned back to where she still sat, looking forlorn. I sighed, giving in, and lowered my glove to let her crawl on for the long ride back. The little rascal had worked hard to drag the heavy glove so far, and I guessed she deserved a ride.

She really did seem to have a great sense of fun about her. She played for hours by herself on the brick patio, spending her time exploring the bags of peat moss and plant pots I had left outside, in case I found time to have a garden.

One day, while I was puttering away outside, I watched as she wrestled and rolled around in a large black empty plastic pot until it finally tipped over. She was inside of it as it started rolling. It gained momentum on the smooth brick, gained height as it bounced over the hard-packed slope, gained speed as it headed down towards the beaver pond, hit a bump, went airborne and then hit the rock retaining wall at the edge of the lawn. All the time it was rolling I could hear "hink hink hink" as it was airborne, "*hoot hoot hoot*," then a momentary silence after it hit the rock wall with a thud. A dizzy little porcupette staggered out. "Hick hick hick." After a few wobbly moments, she regained her thoughts and balance and galloped back up the hill toward me. I approached her thinking she needed comforting, until I realized she was heading for another pot, obviously wanting to repeat the performance, which she did. Later, when I gathered the scattered pots from the hillside, I glanced inside the first pot and burst out laughing. With her little quills lining the inside, it looked like one of those brushes for cleaning the terminals on a car battery.

She would also spend hours tugging and slapping her paws and tail at a piece of corrugated cardboard draped over the side of an unused doghouse. As it flapped in the breeze, she would pretend to quill it. All the while, she would be twirling and spinning around the cardboard, chattering her teeth. This activity also had little diversions, where she scrabbled up the side of the wooden doghouse and peered myopically about her domain.

She was easy to feed. She took immediately to the rodent block, a nutritious commercially prepared kibble that makes up a good portion of the diet I provide for beavers, hares, both red and flying squirrels, my domestic rabbits, mice, and chinchilla. They all seem to prefer a particular brand with lower protein content, and will shun their dish if the wrong brand is presented.

The rest of her diet varied: clover, grasses, fireweed, strawberry plants and fruit, raspberry plants and fruit, apple slices, grapes, cherries, plums, branches from aspen, red and jack pine, lichens, and her favourite treat: yogourt. Fruit treats were given in moderation to protect her digestive system, but she must have had an iron constitution as she never seemed to develop diarrhea or tummy problems. And she loved her water. She would drink deeply, especially after feasting on her rodent block. After drinking she lay in the dish, her scantily furred tummy dipped in the water, and her back pelage spread out over her in a dome, looking very much like a terrestrial sea urchin.

The hair on her back was long, dense, and coarse, while the fur on her face and tummy was fine, sparse, and short. The hair of a young porcupine is initially coal-black, and as the protective quills grow in, a white pattern forms that closely resembles the white stripes of skunks. The *National Audubon Society Field Guide to North American Mammals* states this "contrasting black-and-white 'warning' pattern is not as obvious as that of a skunk, yet in the same way it apparently communicates to a potential adversary that it should keep its distance. The porcupine attempts to keep the black-and-white warning coloration of its backside toward potential enemies." The *Guide* further describes the release of a pungent odour the porcupine releases that can make the attackers' eyes water. The odour did not seem threatening to me, more like a blend of eucalyptus and horse sweat. Not that scary at all. Perhaps the evolution of these animals was aided by this similarity to their pungent counterpart. Porcupines have such low reproductive capacity, slow movement, and docile, trusting personalities, that they are prone to population collapses. Any added dissuasion to predators such as mimicking their smelly, more prolific neighbour, the skunk, would be an aid to their survival.

This mimicry doesn't, however, protect them from the fierce intolerance many humans have towards them. Dog owners whose pets have dared venture too close, horse owners whose harnesses have been chewed to bits, highway maintenance crews who must replace guardrails as these little salt-seekers render them unsafe—all seem to have a bad feeling about porcupines.

A friend raised on a farm in Saskatchewan could not understand why I would even attempt to raise a porcupine.

"You see one, you kill it! Case closed!" she explained.

Not that she had dogs or horses or any special reason for this bias. It was a porcupine, and as far as she was concerned, this attitude, instilled in her by her parents, was the way all people should think.

Another group who seek out this unique creature are members of the First Nations community, who value porcupine quills for cultural art and quillwork. Some of these artisans have taken the progressive, humane initiative to treat the porcupine as a renewable source of quills. Instead of killing the hapless source as is all too frequently done, a few innovative souls have devised a long paddle, made from Styrofoam, which, once a porcupine is found and in a defensive position, is dragged across its back and tail. The quills embed and can easily be stored, stuck in the paddle until needed to produce beautiful quillwork on leather or birch bark. Some folks have even used the long, Styrofoam swimming floats made for children's water play to remove quills. (I think this may be a solution to dog owners who don't want to risk their dogs, but don't want to destroy a porcupine that has been hanging around. Quick, partial dequilling may be all that's required.)

Once P'silla was old enough to be left unattended she spent the day swinging, climbing, and playing in an empty hawk flight pen near the edge of the pond. I had filled the pen with driftwood pieces, dead logs, freshly hewn trees, fresh branches, bags of clean leaves, and an abundance of organic matter I hoped she would find interesting. She had such a calm, easygoing way about her that I was surprised to hear her scream angrily one evening. I rushed down to the pen to find that Cameron the beaver had the fencing in his hands and was shaking it vigorously. P'silla was hanging tenaciously on to the inside of the pen, looking like a kid on a carnival ride. Seeing me, Cameron paused mid-pull and "whee'd," while checking me over for a possible treat. Seeing and smelling none, he gave a final pull and snap of the fencing and turned back to the pond.

The final snap was enough to dislodge the porcupine and she was lobbed like a stone from a slingshot. She righted herself, staggering, and hink-hinked into her little den. When she fell on her back, she had speared dead leaves, dried bark, and even a piece of lettuce. In order to preserve the remainder of her pride, I held back my laughter at the sight, until she had disappeared into her sanctuary. Her decorations remained firmly impaled as she squeezed out of sight. Oh well, I thought, at least she could snack while she sulked.

Later that summer a photographer was sent to take pictures of P'silla for a magazine article about wildlife rehabilitation. I had to keep the animals' daily ritual as normal as possible without exposing them to direct contact with the visitor. As the photographer and I watched, little P'silla, oblivious to our attention, swung, hung, chewed, and played on the driftwood and beaver chew gym, all the time humming to herself. I had set up this woody play area on the gentle slope to the pond, where the light was suitable for photographs. We wanted P'silla to go about her normal exercises, without our presence affecting her behaviour. I kept one eye on the pond in hopes of stopping Cameron mid-rush when he came to greet the newcomer and confront P'silla. Cameron didn't like guys and tried to put the run on any strange man he saw around the place. Only Bruce was tolerated and even he was still eyed suspiciously.

A rustle and a hiss from behind alerted me in time to step between the photographer and the jealous beaver just in time to divert Cameron's charge. But it seemed Cameron was focused on P'silla, who now had ownership of some of his beaver chews in her jungle gym. Cameron gripped my pant leg with an iron fist, peering around my legs while drooling thoughtfully at the photo shoot on the hillside. As he made ready to start hauling his lumber back to the pond, despite the fact there was a small porcupine clinging to it, I had to intervene. Luckily, I had come prepared for such a situation and was able to convince the big beaver to go back to the pond with an apple while the photo shoot continued.

Of course when it was time for the photographer to take some photos of Cameron, the spiteful beaver would have nothing to do with him and swam off in a huff. The young photographer held up pretty well, considering. I think when he originally accepted this assignment he thought he was dealing with trained zoo animals, not animals in training to be wild.

I should explain that a visit to my rehab centre from anyone other than a trained wildlife rehabilitator is not a common or encouraged event. But this was an opportunity for me and for the journalist writing the article to present information to the public regarding the impacts of humans on wildlife and their young. By educating others—explaining what to do, what not to do, and when to get involved—I hoped to stop someone, somewhere, from orphaning a young animal. The porcupette's story was a good example, as it was a cottager intent on saving his trees who had shot her mother. There were other methods of discouragement he could have tried first, such as kids' water guns or even spray from a garden hose, which would probably have sent her packing. Porcupines discourage easily and she would have likely left for good in order to protect her young.

I was fortunate that P'silla was undemanding and easy to care for, because the young fawn that came to my facility shortly after the little porcupine was settled in would keep me hopping for some time.

# Oh, Deer, What Can I Do?

Every summer, I get a call I dread, a call in which I have to explain I can't help out this time. After which I inevitably harbour guilty feelings for a long time. My immediate response to the foreboding call this time was firm and decisive.

"I'm really sorry, ma'am, but I'm afraid I can't accept this one. The best thing is to get the fellow who picked it up to put it back in the same area he found it. The fawn will find the doe once it can hear or smell her."

"Okay," she said, "I'll try to convince him, but he's already had it for a few days, and it's got the runs really bad. I'll clean it up as best I can first, and tell him to take it back."

"Did he feed it cow's milk?" When I heard the affirmative to this question, I cringed. It would likely die from bloat. Even if it were returned to its mother with digestive problems, chances were it would not survive.

I hung up the telephone and spent a guilt-ridden night tossing and turning. I even felt anger towards the misguided rescuer for putting me into this mode of guilt. The fellow who picked up the fawn thought he had actually rescued it and could now raise it as a pet. I suppose once the young deer was messy and sickly, he realized it wasn't fun anymore. He passed the responsibility of its life on to my caller and this kind-hearted lady had a much better sense of what a fawn needed. She quickly realized the young animal was in serious trouble.

My hesitation about taking in the fawn was based on the fact that both my husband and I had just come out of yet another long and demoralizing labour strike. I simply didn't have the money to purchase the litres and litres of goat's milk required to bring it to full growth. If this fawn required the same amount of attention as Beeper, a fawn I had raised and released a few years back, I wasn't sure I had the resources or the energy to raise it.

But right now, only P'silla was requiring special care, and even so she was pretty easy to look after. The other patients in my care were adults. They only needed daily food and water and time to heal their broken bones.

"Oh, what the heck," I groaned.

Rising from a bad night's sleep, I hesitated a moment beside the telephone, and then made the call.

"Oh, thank you, Lil," the woman on the other end of the line said, "I didn't sleep at all last night worrying about the little mite. It doesn't seem to be doing too well, and I'm sure it will just die if we leave it in the bush now." I agreed with her. The fawn had suffered with diarrhea too long, and for that matter, the doe's milk might have already started to dry up. The first few days of separation would have caused the mother a great deal of discomfort, as her udders would be full. This may have incited her to frantically look and call for the missing fawn. But when there isn't a fawn nursing, the need to let down milk quickly wanes. Shortly after, milk production ceases entirely. This scenario played through my mind during the night. By dawn, I had concluded I would give the fawn a chance. By the end of our morning conversation, the woman from Nestor Falls and I had arranged to meet. I would take over the care and feeding of one white-tailed deer fawn.

Most deer give birth in May. However, in years when the previous autumn had been long and warm with lots of succulent foods available, female fawns, then only about eight months old, can actually come into estrus and breed, if they are of sufficient body weight. This almost always occurs at the extreme end of the breeding cycle. While the majority of adult does are bred in November, fawns aren't bred until December or early January. Late breeding means a late summer birthing, sometimes as late as August.

This particular fawn appeared to have been born in early June, only slightly later than most, but it was certainly tiny compared to the ones I had already seen moving about with their mothers in our field. She was likely less than a week old, having been kidnapped within the first day or two of her life. This was bad. It meant she wouldn't have had the full benefit of the doe's colostrum, which is so important for developing immune systems.

The tiny doe fawn stood fifteen inches high from the flat portion of its head to the bottom of its hoof and was fifteen inches long from the tip of its nose to its tail base. Its bony little body weighed a mere six and a half pounds. The caller had kept it hydrated by offering it plain water, a wise choice. The membranes of its tiny mouth and those around its eyes were still soft and moist—a good sign. It felt comfortably warm to touch, also a good thing. Soft, dappled skin hung loosely off its diminutive hips and ribs, a less promising sign. We had arranged to meet at the vet clinic in Kenora, where Dr. Christiansen gave it a thorough examination. She determined it was healthy enough, though she was worried that the scours, a digestive disorder common to ruminants, would become our biggest battle.

Now, I had to find a diet it could digest. Ideally, the only thing I should have offered it was fresh goat's milk. Unfortunately, there was no goat's milk, fresh or powder, farm-raised or store-bought, available to me at that time in Kenora. My second choice would have been a commercial lamb's product, but it was long past lambing season, and there was not an animal feed store within at least a couple of hundred miles with a bag left. I was forced to use a cow calf milk-replacement powder, which I did have in stock. I reluctantly mixed a bit of this into an electrolyte formula, producing a dilute mixture.

I figured if the fawn's digestive system stabilized, I could gradually increase the concentration of milk-replacer in the formula but for now electrolytes were important to counter the effects of the diarrhea.

She readily took this sweet-smelling mix, draining the bottle completely. Tail twitching frantically, she bleated and bunted the empty bottle for more, pawing at me with tiny legs.

I resisted the temptation to feed her more, secretly wanting to see a satisfying bulge in her little tummy, but I knew better. I reluctantly ignored her nudges for more. It is too easy to lose babies to bloat from overfeeding, especially on a new or unnatural diet.

Sure enough, her digestive system immediately reacted, growling, gurgling, and rumbling. Within minutes, I had to contend with the remnants of her last cow's milk meal on me, on her, on the mat, even on the wall. She was weak and shaky after this gastric indignity, but decidedly more comfortable. I wiped her down with a moist cloth before she tottered into the darkness of a large pet carrier I had padded with blankets and hot water bottles. After a few curious sniffs at the scent memories left by past tenants, she arched her back stiffly, stretched her legs and lay down, coiling into a pie-sized ball of fur.

Later, I would have to find a spot for her to stay outside where she would be warm, safe, and not in contact with the smells and sounds of humans or pets. But outside housing wasn't an option just then, as the recent nights had been cold and wet. I padded the floor of my rehab room, having decided to feed her there. The pet carrier, lined with hot water bottles and soft burlap padding, would provide the warm, dark solitude she had sought after her meal and upset tummy.

After this first feeding, I left her on her own, grooming herself and generally behaving in a fashion that seemed very mature for her age. No crying for companionship, or seeking my body heat.

I figured that if I could stabilize her, I would make arrangements to ship her off to a wildlife rehabilitation centre specializing in raising fawns. However, I was to find out the new, strict rules on release and relocation of animals had narrowed down the choices I once had available to me. A barrage of hoops and legal barriers now existed to prevent the moving of large, wild animals. Regulations dictate that once they are ready for release, they must be returned to their original location. The wildlife custodian I had chosen was located at the other end of the province, the same ones to whom Brownie the moose calf had been sent. I knew Christine and Pete would face great problems trying to return the deer back to me for release, if they were to decide to take it.

While I was experienced at raising fawns, I did not have ungulates on my wildlife custodian licence at this time. I could not afford the extensive, expensive pens and fencing which were mandatory under my licence if I were to try to house a young one. But I'd cross that bridge later; for now, I'd just worry about getting it strong.

That meant feedings day and night. This created a problem, since I worked in town during the day. Total travel time, to come home, feed her, and return to work would have been over two hours, meaning that I would be very late returning to my job. Solutions to my problems seem to miraculously appear sometimes, and this was one of those times. A neighbour and friend to whom I had explained my plight offered to take on the daytime feedings. I'm quite particular about who comes into contact with animals I am raising. It takes a certain presence and voice to calm and reassure wild animals. Kathy was a perfect choice. Her nursing experience, complemented by a wildlife rehabilitation training course, made her a suitable volunteer. She was also committed to keeping animals wild. Under her care, I knew there would be no extra patting, handling or talking to the fawn, something I know is hard to refrain from doing as they are so darn cute.

The fawn's scours continued into the next evening. Despite her gastric problems, she still fed enthusiastically. But because of the continuing diarrhea, her bottle consisted mostly of electrolyte solution. She was hungry and thin. She needed more substantial nutrition, yet she just couldn't handle it. She would wail piteously, trying to coax something better from her bottle, flailing at me with her little hooves.

On the third evening of my care, the temperature was warm enough to let her go outside on the lawn. I welcomed this change of venue, as this would mean fewer cleanups for me once her stomach reacted to the food. And since I had increased the concentration of formula into the electrolytes again, I was quite certain there would be a reaction. So for the first time, I fed her outside. After her frenzied attempts at satiation from the bottle, her tummy growled ominously. She licked at her side frantically, obviously uncomfortable and gassy. Then she did a strange thing—she sniffed long and hard, eyes closed dreamily, nose up, facing the beaver pond. I thought for a moment that she was having a seizure. On wobbly legs, she tottered towards the soft shores of the pond, sniffing here and there, searching. Ignoring the mud sucking at her little hooves, she wobbled out to a clay upwelling in the shallow water. After a satisfied sniff at the exposed clay, she started to lick and chew at it. My first impulse, was to cry, "No, yucky!" to her, but I then remembered the calf moose Brownie and Cameron the beaver. Of course. Maybe one of these days I'd catch on. She, too, was hardwired to know what she needed. And, me, I'm too hardwired as a human, automatically thinking that mud and dirt is bad and I should try to keep little animals from eating it. The stuff she ate now, the raw version of Kaopectate, kaolin or clay, would help her stomach. After consuming a considerable amount she sniffed her way over to a pile of organic muck that had been pushed up by the beavers. She sorted through the pile with her nose, excited and frantic, and then she began to swallow disgustingly slimy pieces of who knows what.

The swiftness of the cure was incredible, as it had been with Brownie and Cameron. Although the clay quickly passed through her digestive system, there was no undigested formula with it. The organic material held the cure that her digestive system needed.

As early as the next morning her stools started to have the consistency they should, though they were clay-coloured. By the following evening, she was able to eat her formula full-strength, with no tummy turbulence. She slept soundly and comfortably all that night.

The week passed without further incident. A convenient pattern developed. The fawn would spend its time curled up in the carrier, sleeping or lying incredibly still. Only its shiny black nose moved, nostrils flaring, taking in new scents. It would remain tightly curled until either Kathy or I gave a soft doe-call, summoning it for food.

Her wakeup ritual was always the same. Bum up first, and then the little toothpick front legs would unfold, followed by an incredibly perfect stiff-legged arch. With the tiny tail curling over her back, she would utter a little "meep" and out she would trot. After a few head-butts in inappropriate, tender parts of the human anatomy, she would focus on the bottle. As she locked on, with lips and tongue curling around and sealing the nipple, the bottle would collapse as it swiftly emptied. As she fed, her tail switched back and forth frantically. This white-flagged signal meant we needed to contend with that end too.

A warm damp cloth took the place of mom when it came to the fawn's toilet. In the wild, does consume these tiny, shiny offerings to ensure that no scent from fawns lingers for predators to detect. I was quite a bit less dedicated, or at least had a different perspective than her real mom would have had, but I did have access to washcloths and waste buckets for depositing such goodies. If she did not require such services, she would flatten her little tail down tightly which I took to mean "never mind, thank you very much."

By the second week, the weather warmed enough to think about keeping her outside. I was adamant that if I did have to raise her, I would do everything possible to give her a chance at living wild. But a single, human-fostered fawn is not a good candidate for successful release.

The large kennel that had been Cameron's outside protection was still set up on dry ground. A tarp covered it, which would provide weather protection. To complete her new home I used bales of straw, broken and whole, to line the edges. Large evergreen branches were added to form darkened pseudo-canopies in the corners.

She was still at the stage when she would seek a dark spot to bed down after feeding, so now she was quite content within the security of her new pen. She was so adept at hiding in it that at first glance I often could not see where she was bedded unless I had watched her go. She could flatten into the branches, between the bales, or under the straw so effectively that nothing belied her position. Until I made the soft doe-call, and the answering "meep" came, I wondered time and again whether she had escaped the pen. But no, a rustle of hay, the mandatory stretch and out she would come. She seemed content and stayed in the compound for the following week without complaint.

So undetectable was she when she bedded down in the pen that it almost cost her life. Bruce, having come home for the weekend, decided to do battle with our wayward lawn. He hadn't seen the fawn in the compound and assumed that I had moved it or had it with me in the big field.

During the first few passes with the riding lawn mower, she remained hidden, but then on another, too-close drive-by, the fawn panicked, hitting the kennel wire full-tilt. Her little head went through the wiring and she hung there, stunned. Bruce had heard nothing over the roar of the lawnmower and was unaware of what had happened. I heard only a faint bleat of pain, then silence. I raced across the field to her side and managed to free her before she strangled or broke her neck.

Bruce was devastated when he realized what had happened. "Oh, Lil, I didn't think she was there … I'm so sorry!"

We were all pretty shaken from this ordeal. I put her in the small carrier to calm her down. I had to figure out something safer for her. I knew I couldn't count on confining her in the outside compound any longer. If a bear or fox tried to get at her when I wasn't home, she could easily panic and kill herself in the wire fence, trying to flee the predator.

Every day after her feeding, she would wander further and further from where I watched, moving cautiously around the pond's edge, tasting and testing everything. Unlike Beeper, she did not want to be with me and was extremely independent and elusive. If I didn't watch her closely, she would eventually melt away to bed down in the sedges that grew in a thick patch alongside the beaver pond next to the lawn. The first time I lost sight of where she had disappeared to I panicked and searched the grasses to no avail. Even my "meeping" calls, which usually brought her running, wouldn't budge her out of her hiding spot, presumably because her tummy was full. Once hidden, she was lost to my eyes until the next feeding. Sure enough, when feeding time came, I walked to the edge of the pond, "meeped," and out she raced to get her milk meal. I rationalized that if she did sneak off like that in the morning or during the day it was okay, even a good thing. The nights however were a different matter, as the predators travelled under the cover of darkness. And the surrounding forest was filled with foxes and bears; for that matter, even a hungry mink could take down this tiny little mite. But her being free eliminated my fear of her being hurt in the outside pen, so I reluctantly accepted her independence, believing that it was the best solution to a dangerous situation.

Her show of self-determination was encouraging. After the morning feeding, I would leave a note for Kathy saying which direction the fawn had wandered into the sedges, and when Kathy came for the daytime feedings she would stand on the lawn and give a doe-call. Within minutes the fawn emerged, head tossing and tail twitching. After feeding, the fawn melted into the grasses again, and no amount of calling or searching would reveal her presence.

More than once I followed quietly behind her in hopes of seeing where she went to bed down. The tall sedges were chest height on me, and if I crouched I could enter the awesome, green-tinted underworld she sought. The dense sedge covering, which looked like a moving green sea from above, provided complete cover from the sun. Trails and paths left by beavers and muskrats wound through the tussocks, free from undergrowth. Snaps and pops above me, along with the occasional scurry of scratchy legs across my neck, announced the presence of grasshoppers, upset at having been disturbed from their hiding spots. As they dropped to the ground, large leopard frogs or members of the microtine world quickly snapped them up. Voles and mice would look up from their struggling meal, shocked by my intrusion, and dart into a tussock for a further layer of protection. The fawn's dainty tracks were evident on the beaver and muskrat trails, indicating her course, but she could always elude me. After every fruitless search I slunk back to my own world and left her where she felt secure.

Windy days were different, though. Her green sea parted in the winds, exposing the browned tussocks beneath the green sheaves, the persistent remnants from previous years of growth. Then there was little cover to seek in the sedge sea, so as an alternative she sought a tangled patch of beaked hazel, raspberries, viburnums, and alders near the old house. Even in this seemingly open cover she would disappear as if by magic, her dappled coat absorbing the light and colours of the leaves. When it was windy she was nervous and jumpy, and would often not come out for her feeding until the winds subsided in the evening. She did the same on stormy days, which I must admit I appreciated. One close call in a lightning storm with the moose calf was enough for me.

Still fretting about her food, I was finally able to purchase a supply of powdered goat's milk. The local supermarket had just restocked their shelves of this rare commodity and its timely availability was much appreciated. The goat's milk, with pediatric supplements added, mixed into a suitably rich, nutritious diet for her. She filled out and grew, though slowly. I observed that wild fawns, even those I believed had been born late in the year, were noticeably larger than she. Still, as a month and then five weeks went by, she filled out, muscle mass developed on her tiny haunches, and her bones became strong and sturdy. But she seemed dwarfed. Her poor start in life was telling. By August she was browsing more and more, selecting choice leaves and grasses. Her sensitive nose and lips would part the turf, bypassing rich clovers to select a certain patch of thin wiry grass called toad rush. The seed pods of these grasses held a sweet, milky starch. Come fall, after the first few touches of frost sweetened the leaves, clover would be more to her liking, but not yet. Her nimble lips could take off a single raspberry, leaving its unripe neighbour untouched. She nipped the flowers of the white-and-blue asters in the field, pulled off the older strawberry leaves, yet left the young centres unscathed. For some reason, if a plant had a damaged or discoloured leaf, she would sniff and select it over the healthy ones. It was as if whatever compounds the plant sent to heal or protect its damaged part carried a different scent or aura she preferred.

She wanted me to be around when she browsed in the field, as a lookout for danger, I presumed. Thus engaged, she would occasionally signal to me from where she browsed with a head toss or tail twitch. I would use a side-to-side twitch of my hand, or my light-coloured work glove, to signal all was well. It was so neat to watch how she tried communicating with tail switches and foot and leg positions and I was keen to learn the subtle differences in her body language. For example, while I normally lept Brill and Heidi well away from the fawn I still had to rely on the dogs to be on guard for bears. One evening while Brill sat watching from the hillside, the fawn suddenly noticed her. Her tail went straight into the air and bristled to its full flare. Her head went up as far as her slender neck would hold it and her ears went forward. But it was her footwork that was most fascinating She started a high-stepping walk, bringing her foot down in a tiny stomp and then a pause. As she moved she continued to stare at the dog, but when she paused she turned to stare directly at my feet. Then I figured it out. She was waiting for me to signal to her whether the dog was safe to approach. I had to think of what the right response to give her would be, trying to remember what does do when they flee. So I tried a foot stomp and flashed my gloved hand down as if I were a doe covering her white tail. That was it! Off she flew, snorting and blowing. I think I had successfully communicated to her that dogs were not her friends.

Or maybe I had just told her there was a sale on bananas at the local super-market. I'm not sure what it translated to, but it sure produced a reaction.

Outings with the fawn provided great opportunities for me to get a moment's respite from the more mundane chores. Slathered in bug repellant and armed with bear spray, I would sit and read a good book while she browsed, an indulgence not often available to me.

One warm, calm evening, amid the drone of mosquitoes, I settled back against a spruce in the field and eagerly started into a new mystery novel. It was a great read and set in our local area, so I could relate to the character's movements and locations. Partway into the novel I came across the name Persephone. This nudged my too-distant memories of Greek mythology and I tried to remember why the name seemed appropriate now.

Watching the fawn bathed in the soft light, blissfully nipping off and eating wildflowers, brought back to me the story of the goddess Demeter, who could control the seasons. Her daughter Persephone was enamoured of flowers, and, as the story goes, could not return to her world of gods and goddesses after she ate the foods—pomegranate seeds—of the netherworld. I guess the fawn's initial meal of cow's milk made her a Persephone of the human world.

Now that Cameron was living free, our contact with each other was limited to a quick exchange of greetings and a treat when we met on the shore of the pond. I still watched his interactions and noted his developing skills, but I didn't pick him up or touch him anymore. In any case I don't think I could have as he was now well over sixty pounds. He would swim back and forth in the pond watching as I fed P'silla or Persephone, wheezing an occasional greeting.

Sometimes after feeding the fawn I would set down her bottle and go back into the house for something else I needed. When I returned the bottle would be gone, and I would later find its remnants, chewed beyond recognition, floating at the pond's edge. I should have known better. Watering dishes, rubber gloves, towels—all disappeared mysteriously into the watery depths, only to wash up on shore in tatters and barely recognizable. It seemed that as long as my scent was on it, it was fair game for Cameron.

He seemed to feel it was his job to torment the little creatures that ventured near his shores. Poor Persephone was badly scared more than once when she wandered into the pond to indulge in geophagy. She continued to eat dirt for her stomach problems so despite Cameron's bullying she would bravely, albeit cautiously, work her way to the muddy shoreline of her choice. I would keep watch over her and scan the waters for any sign of Cameron. Sometimes there was only a ripple; other times there was a wake that would put a cruising crocodile to shame. Sometimes when the apex of a wake reached the shallows Cameron erupted from the water, lunging at the fawn. Maybe I really had been watching too many *National Geographic* shows, but it sure seemed like a boreal forest rendition of a scene from the Serengeti, with gnus and crocodiles being substituted with fawns and beavers.

Soon, though, the fawn ignored his bluffs. She would stare him down with her back arched, tail up and hoof mid-air, as he hissed and puffed. His intimidations no longer effective, Cameron would give up and leave. If she stopped to nibble at his treats, though, another attack would ensue.

When Brownie and Eh the beaver had their face-to-face encounter, I had not been armed with a camera. With Persephone and Cameron ,though, I was fortunate enough to capture on film a couple of these remarkable encounters. I had also learned to stand far enough back to avoid the inevitable spray of muddy water.

# Freedom for P'silla

Rehabilitators raising orphaned or kidnapped babies need to have a good intuition about when the young animal is actually ready for release. When feeding the very young, for example, we must make sure we wean them from liquids to solids gradually. We have to be sure we know when they are ready, not just that we want them to be ready, perhaps to make space for a newcomer to the facility. Since human caregivers aren't a natural parent to such animals, we may not be able to give them everything they need. Because of that, normal development of the animal may not be achieved, which means maturation can be delayed. Fortunately, baby animals are so hardwired to become independent they will usually make the milestone decisions required for survival themselves. And we as rehabilitators just have to be able to correctly interpret the signs.

For example, I wasn't certain what would determine when and whether P'silla was ready to go it on her own. I intended to release her mid-August, but she seemed very babyish and not prepared for total independence. I continued to watch for signs of maturity. One of her first big achievements was developing the ability to debark the branches I provided. Next I monitored her incisor development, and when they turned from milky white to oxidized orange, another milestone was reached. Then I noticed a new band of quills growing where they had not existed before. Short, sturdy projections developed around her neck and head, armouring what had once been a very vulnerable spot. By now she could climb trees quickly and could cling to limbs tenaciously as she chewed on the bark. At any real or perceived threat, she would flare her quills and burrow her more vulnerable head and neck into a crevice or hole. Now I believed she was ready to go out on her own.

Bruce and I had explored possible areas for release. To return her to the cottage area where she originated we thought would only put her in contact with some who were more likely to kill her. After all, they had killed her mother.

I knew of an area not too far from where she had been rescued but hopefully far enough to ensure her safety, where only a few hunters and a registered trapper ventured. Debarked Jack pines announced the presence of other porkies, which in my mind made the site all that more appealing. It would be as safe as any, I supposed.

I listened to the local weather reports and the next storm-free weekend Bruce and I planned our trip. My first concern was to get P'silla into her kennel. I hadn't handled her in weeks as her quills were long, hard, and sharp. She could do me serious damage now if she decided she didn't like my groping. As with the young beavers, I had always convinced P'silla to climb into a basket or kennel when I needed to transport her from place to place around the yard, so I hoped she would still cooperate. Sure enough, with the added enticement of a banana P'silla willingly climbed into the shaving-filled carrier and, humming to herself, made herself comfortable and proceeded to devour the banana. I had also added a dish of rodent block, plums, grapes, and apple to the carrier, intending to leave both P'silla and the food at the release site along with a full water dish.

We drove a rocky, bumpy pipeline access road for what seemed like hours. There were times when all three of us were bounced high off our seats and into the air, despite seat belts or bungee cord restraints.

After a gruelling ride, Bruce said, "This looks great here, Lil."

There were large crevices in fractured bedrock, which angled down several metres, and piles and piles of broken rock, creating multiple hiding and sleeping places for security-seeking porcupines. Nearby there were thick and fresh clover patches, both young and old stands of Jack pine, a marsh, and a shallow pond ringed with a variety of aquatic vegetation. Best of all, not too far away we had seen signs of another porcupine. We hoped P'silla's presence wouldn't be viewed by the resident porkies as an intrusion. I was sure vocal contact with others of her species during the still of the night would be a good thing.

We weren't too sure how she had fared during the bumpy ride but our concerns abated when we unloaded the carrier and peered in. Her response to our intrusion was a soft "hink hink." I gave her a drink of water and then searched the carrier for the extra food I had packed in it, only to find it was all gone. Obviously she hadn't stressed out during the bumpy trip, as she had eaten everything.

Bruce lugged the carrier and its curious passenger up to one of the rock crevices closest to the forest edge. When we opened the door, P'silla romped over to the largest crack in the rock, paused, took a deep sniff, and then crawled down into the darkness. As she came to a small break in the rock wall, she squeezed into it and flared her quills, effectively sealing the entrance. Then she relaxed, pulled herself through the crack, and proceeded deeper into the rock. She repeated this trick a couple of times before turning around and coming back out to us. I was worried she was going to want to crawl back into the carrier, but no, she passed us by and ambled over to another crevice with a different rock formation. She proceeded to test her teeth on chunks of dry wood and branches, which had accumulated in the crevice over the years. Then she started to buck and romp back and forth, in and out of each opening and pathway, apparently thrilled with what she saw. As entertaining as this was for us, it was time for us to head home.

Yet I couldn't leave her without providing her with a final treat. After filling a large water dish so she wouldn't have to venture down to the pond for a drink until she got her bearings, I pulled a banana and apple out of my own lunch. I tucked it under a rock overhang for her to find, out of sight of scavenging ravens. As we drove off, I could see her stretched out on a large flat rock, munching on an apple, a dark cave behind her. I thought her feeding spot might have been her version of a deck or patio.

I could only hope that she had a chance to be a normal little porcupine. Literature says that October is the porcupine's breeding season, and although she was too young, she would likely hear and encounter other porcupines

during their time of movement and socializing. I didn't want to think about whatever other fate she might meet with in the future. I only know that sometimes I am more than a little dismayed when I see licensed, trained hunters, who would normally show respect and restraint while hunting big game, regress to the disgusting deed of killing animals they have no intention of eating, for the fun of it. Under specific conditions, it is legal for landowners to humanely dispatch certain species of animals to protect their property. In my opinion a bit of bark removal does not warrant a death sentence.

There are licence requirements, quotas, and management strategies in place to ensure big game species and furbearing mammals are managed with respect, but for a number of relatively harmless species, including the porcupine, no such protection exists. Not too long ago, while Bruce was shopping in a sporting goods store in a small tourist community nearby, I passed time by scanning the walls of the store looking at the various mounted specimens hanging there. In amongst the glassy eyes and cobwebbed antlers, a photo of a grinning hunter holding a dead, bloodied porcupine impaled on the end of a stick struck me as obscene and disgusting. While I am sure the flesh of the deer and moose whose stuffed heads hung on the shop's walls at least fed some families, the porcupine was killed merely for sport. Evidently, the hunter agreed with that belief I had heard from my friend: "You see one, you kill it! Case closed!"

I knew how lucky I was to have had the experience of observing and knowing this uncommon, relatively secretive little animal. I hope that perhaps by telling the story of this particular little porcupine, the innocent victim of a human being preoccupied with meeting his own needs, I may prevent a similar outcome in the future.

# Bear Trouble

The cooler days of late summer initiated a flurry of activity in the beaver pond. Amongst the excited and noisy ducks and geese, the beavers
quietly toiled. Cutting and chipping, clipping and hauling, they slowly created clearings within the once-dense aspen stands. I appreciated their daytime presence when I was outside working, as I relied on their extra sets of
eyes and—more importantly—noses to warn me when the bears made their
rounds searching for easy food. Many times while I was with Persephone as
she browsed in the field, the beavers would start slapping their tails in frantic
warnings. This was my cue to grab my stuff, shoo the fawn into thick cover
and head home, usually just in time to catch a glimpse of a bear sidling around
the pond.

I was always relieved when the bear proved to be a small sow or a yearling, instead of the massive boar, or male bear, that had gone on a spree of killing and destruction at our home earlier in the year. That horrible experience
had left me nervous and jumpy all summer. Now that fall was near, I thought
there was a good chance that the same bear would be back, looking for food
and causing trouble. He certainly had claimed it as his territory, as boars are

wont to do, by biting off small trees and raking the bark of larger trees with his claws.

Prior to that ugly encounter in the spring when that bear killed several chickens, we seemed to have an uneasy peace with the other, smaller bears. They seemed content to feed along the nearby ponds and roadsides, satisfied with lush clover and berries to fill their bellies. These bears had their regular trails, and as long as I kept the household garbage cans empty and cleaned up, and the eagle pens free of fish and animal parts, they would continue on their way, going about their business without incident. But finally, one hot summer evening, I should have known something more dangerous than usual was around that night, as the resident animals, wild and domestic, were giving signals of fear.

The beavers were tail-slapping long, loud warnings as I gave my wards their evening meal. I watched the field nervously, half-expecting to see a bear appear at any minute. Two deer burst out of the woods and ran between the house and where I stood, startling me something terrible. They veered past me and raced towards the field, tails flagging as they ran. They ignored my presence and continued blowing their fear at some unseen enemy. When they reached the edge of the field, they stopped and stared back into the woods from where they had come, tails twitching nervously and ears flashing back and forth, before streaking down another trail and out of sight.

Whatever it was that had scared them wasn't very far away, and I had a creepy feeling, as if I were being watched. I was glad when I finished the last of my evening chores, and could retire to the safety of the house before the sun set. The dogs growled softly and paced through the rooms, jumping up to stare out the windows off and on during the night. When I tried to convince them to go out for a bathroom break before I went to bed, they slunk off to hide in the closet instead. While this is the way our dogs had behaved last winter when the wolves were hanging around the field, I didn't think wolves were the cause of their fear this time. Usually, the dogs were a bit braver and more than willing to go out and scream at the bears that ventured into the yard. But not on this particular summer night. They cowered in the darkness of the closet, forsaking their normal sleeping spots at the foot of my bed, whimpering at sounds too faint for my ears.

My sleep was sound and uninterrupted that night, as the dogs didn't wake me to go out. Instead, they stayed in their safe closet den until dawn, with only an occasional soft whimper. I awakened feeling refreshed and eager to start my day. As I stepped outside, the dogs raced past me, then stopped and stood on the deck, sniffing the air and growling. I put Heidi on a leash, and had to pull hard to convince her to come with me as I went up the hill to where my poultry pens were. A massive fresh bear scat lay in the centre of my trail, and feathers floated around in the morning breeze.

Two maimed hens staggered around the shattered remains of the henhouse and cackled in alarm when they saw me. I couldn't believe the mess I saw before me! My poor little egg-layers had been mauled. Most of them were dead, but only partially eaten. The remains of their mangled, lifeless bodies had been pressed flat by the bulk of the bear, as he sat on them to finish his dirty deed.

My pet doe rabbit, who had made her warren in the floor of the hen house, safe from hawks and foxes, hopped forlornly around the scattered debris, sniffing at the many lifeless little bodies. The bear had smelled the baby bunnies, even through the pungent odour of the chicken manure and thick grass and hair cover the doe had bundled them in. He had killed them all, squishing them and leaving their tiny fuzzy bodies flung about the hen house, all mixed up with the dead chickens, all uneaten.

It's common for bears to dig out and eat chipmunks and voles the same size as these little bunnies as a normal part of their diet, but it seemed that this bear's intention was just to kill the babies.

He had moved on to the second chicken coop and killed all of its occupants as well. They were all roosters, from which he ate only the contents of their crops, leaving the once beautiful, proud birds alive but eviscerated, to die slowly on the lawn.

It looked as if he had then climbed on top of the rabbit hutches, ripping apart the doors as he flattened the pens with his weight. The occupants of these pens were half-wild buck rabbits who were able to flee when the doors were ripped off. And flee they did. It took over a week after this episode for them to show themselves to me. I had assumed they were all dead until I finally saw them creeping out from under a brush pile to seek a drink of water.

In addition to the rabbits, a young red squirrel I had housed in an outside pen received a premature release, when the bear ripped off the screen to reach for a small dish of seeds and rodent block. This bear was not starving, as there was ample food available, including all the dead hens—this was just a very nasty rogue bear.

I felt so sorry for my beautiful little hens. Some were very old in hen years, but all were still willing to produce an egg or two a week for me. Mostly, though, they were my favourite agents of biological pest control for the garden. I gently tended to the injuries on the two hens and one rooster, who had survived by somehow managing to escape the bear's attack, and put them into a sturdy dog run. I figured the fencing of the run was as strong as that used for the "bear-proof" communal garbage shed down the road. When I had driven by the garbage shed earlier in the week, I inferred from the large scratches on the door that a bear, likely the same one that had assaulted our yard and my wards, had tried unsuccessfully to enter the shed. If this one was going to return to our place, I hoped he would decide he couldn't get into my newly fenced dog run enclosure, which to me looked reasonably similar to the garbage shed.

A few nights later, the beavers were frantic again, splashing and hissing in the safety of the pond. I heard something splashing through the water, probably a predator trying to get them, and I was quite certain it was a bear. Once again, the dogs hid in the closet.

Early the next morning, I heard a ruckus which I recognized as the sound of chickens in distress. There was a lot of flapping and banging coming from the enclosure I had put the remaining few chickens in, but in the dim morning light, I couldn't see just what was going on. I went out on the deck and hooted and hollered. In the past, yelling had always been enough to send off any bear.

Not so this time.

In the dawn's early light, I saw this massive black shape hurtling up the hill towards me. It slowed its charge when it was beneath the deck where I stood. Growling and popping its jaws, it reared back on its heels, staring up at me.

Whoa! This is getting pretty scary! I thought.

Over the years, when I had wanted to scare other bears out of the yard, if yelling didn't work or move them along fast enough, I would shoot into the ground with a .410 gauge shotgun. The noise and sound of scattered shot had always seemed to be enough to send them on their way in fright. I raced in to the gun safe and fumbled with the lock, hoping the bear would be long gone by the time I figured out the combination.

No such luck. By the time I had secured the shotgun and shells, the boar had circled the house. In retrospect, I'm sure he did this to try to figure how to get up to where I was standing. I felt safer being armed, even though I intended only to scare him with the noise. With this newly acquired bravado, I stepped out the patio door, cautiously peering around after each step, trying to see where he had gone. He suddenly appeared from around the corner of the house, some twenty or thirty paces from me, heading slowly up the hill towards the ravaged pens. Because he hadn't seen me, I felt I could surprise and scare him effectively with the sound of the gun. I took careful aim into a mound of deep soil near the bear, a mound free of rocks and other hard, flat surfaces. I didn't want any stray pellets ricocheting around or to have spent lead landing where the ducks or geese could pick it up.

The gun's retort made me blink and my ears ring. I peered over the balcony, fully expecting to see the south end of a bear going north. But he was still there, stopped and now glaring at me; the sound of the shot and the impact of the pellets in the dirt beside him had not had the desired effect. He began to pace back and forth, as if he was trying to figure how to reach me. My brain, rattled as it was, told me this was now a serious and potentially dangerous situation. I went back into the house to get a rifle of a calibre high enough to dispatch the bear, if necessary. I took a moment to calm down and also to console the dogs, now shrieking their heads off from the safety of the closet. The attitude of this bear was such that I was afraid he might even try to get into the house to attack the dogs—or me!

I pulled my hunting rifle out of the gun safe, fully aware I was taking a drastic step. Even though I feel competent with a firearm, it was times like this that I wished Bruce were at home. I don't do much shooting to kill, and my recent firearm experience had been limited to sighting in my rifle on paper targets in the field. Concentric rings staring back have a milder psychological effect than do the menacing stares of a bear. However, Bruce was at the far end of the province, so it was just me versus *ursus*.

I took a deep breath and stepped out onto the balcony again. I could see him standing on the hill, but trees prevented a clear view and killing shot. It seemed that he had calmed down and was again sniffing the air. I watched from my vantage point on the deck, following his progress as he stuck to the bush line, always partially hidden.

I suppose he wasn't totally satisfied with his earlier destruction, or perhaps he sought leftovers, as he made his towards the remains of the chicken coop. He paused in front of a large flight cage used to house recovering eagles, sniffed, and then ripped off the door.

The flight cage held no eagle then, but did provide temporary quarters to a kit found lying beside its dead mother on a roadway. The remainder of the fox family had escaped unharmed, but this little one had injuries that needed tending to. The injuries were now healed, and the kit was ready to be taken back to its remaining family and den site. As with many wild canids, the male fox would continue to care for his kits, even though their mom was dead. I hoped to reunite this one with the father. But this was not to be. I saw a red blur rip past the legs of the bear, and watched with relief as the kit disappeared into the thick bushes. At least it survived the bear's attack, even if it had a premature release, like that of the squirrel.

The sun had fully risen now, and perhaps feeling more vulnerable in the light of day the bear slunk into the thick, dark forest behind the house. I waited until I heard him crashing well off into the distance before venturing off the deck to take stock of his most recent destruction. I still clutched the rifle and watched the bushes, in case he returned, while I walked over to the pen where I had first seen him that morning.

The fowl that I had moved into what I thought was a safe pen were his most recent victims. The bear had climbed on top of the wiring and pulled open a hole large enough to crawl through. Once again, he ate out only the crop and developing eggs within the body cavity of the hens and tossed aside the "remainders." The rooster also lay dead and flattened.

I had never felt so violated and rattled as I did after this ursine rampage. I trembled and shook for the remainder of the morning, and jumped at every noise. The dogs were also jumpy and they too yelped at sudden sounds, not helping my nerves any. That bear had to go.

I called the city of Kenora bylaw officers, the agents in charge of bear removal in our neighbourhood. Later that day a large live trap, designed specifically to catch nuisance bears, was delivered, set, and baited in our yard. I set up my baby monitors around the perimeter of the yard so that when I was in the house, I would be able to hear when the bear came around and wouldn't be surprised or suddenly confronted by him. If the bear was nearby, I didn't want to walk out at night to tend to a sick animal, or let the dogs out to do their thing. The first night the trap was set it was successful, which let me right a wrong that the bear had caused.

It wasn't the bear that was lured by the sweet-smelling bait springing the trap, but rather a frightened little kit fox, looking for a free meal. I checked for evidence of the now-healed scars, to make sure that it was actually the one the bear had released the night before. Sure enough, there were pale ridges with new hair growing in where the wounds had been. This time I would take no chances of him not being returned to his family. I fed him well, crated him up and drove him the distance to where he had been picked up on the road. I drove into an old gravel pit nearby and was relieved to see fresh fox signs, of both kit and adult. I let him go near a brush pile, into which he immediately darted. He turned around and was peering out, sniffing the air as I returned to the truck. I can only hope he was recognizing familiar scents and that he would be reunited with his family by nightfall, with nothing more than a few bad memories to grow up with. I should be so lucky to only have bad memories to deal with at home.

I was relieved to see the bear trap was still in place when I pulled into the driveway.

A few nights later, Heidi and Brill's angry growling woke me up. The baby monitors were picking up godawful sounds. Not sounds of animals in distress, thank heavens, it was warning tail splashes from the beavers that blasted through the monitors like rifle shots. I also heard a keening sound, loud huffing, and toenails scratching on metal. I deduced that the bear was walking around the trap! After what seemed like forever, I heard the metallic crash of the door, followed by the onslaught of paws, muscle, teeth, and fury on the inner walls of the live trap. And then the bellowing started! Both dogs had darted into the closet by this time, and were huddled in a corner. Magnified through the baby monitors, the sound was ghastly.

"We got 'im, Lil," croaked Bruce.

Bruce had seen the damage the bear had left behind after the rampage; though he had not personally witnessed the bear's fury. Curiosity bettered us so, flashlights in hand, we went outside to take a look at what we had caught and to turn off the outside baby monitors. The flashlight beams illuminated a red-eyed, baleful glare and reflected off shiny but broken yellowed teeth, pulled back into a scary snarl. I had never witnessed a bear snarling before. In the past, the ones I had seen close up had just puckered their lips and popped their jaws. A new and hideous side of bruin life was revealed to me. Shivering, we went back into the house, glad the beast was now securely incarcerated.

Some bears return to their trapped location within days, especially if the trap experience isn't too traumatic for them. I wanted to make sure this bear never, ever wanted to come back to our neighbourhood. So next morning, when I went about my chores and the bear began to growl at me through the metal grating, I hooted and shouted and banged kettles in front of it. I even let the dogs shriek at it, and I splashed it with water. None of my antics had any discernible effect on the bear. It didn't withdraw to the back of the trap; it didn't blink; it just glared. Then it reached down and with its teeth slowly ripped off a chunk from the side of the heavy plastic bait pail, momentarily held it, then spit the plastic out, never breaking the baleful gaze boring into me.

Hoo, boy, I said to myself, thoroughly creeped out. I began to worry whether he might come back. I couldn't help but think he looked bent on revenge.

I was relieved when the bylaw officers hooked the trap to their vehicle to haul him away. His red-eyed, menacing stare remained burned in my mind long after they left.

A week or so later Bruce and I woke to the sound of the compost bin being tipped over. I peeked out the bedroom window and my eyes met those of a black bear, with some disgusting, dripping thing in its mouth.

Oh, no! I thought, he's back! But then I realized what I was looking at was a smaller bear with the daintier features of a female.

"Bruce," I whispered, "there's a bear in the compost!"

Bruce jumped up and retrieved his 12-gauge shotgun and the box of special rubber bullets given to us by the Ministry of Natural Resources. A hit with a rubber bullet would hurt and scare a bear, but wouldn't maim or kill it. He pulled out the little .410 from the vault as well.

He hesitated before asking, "Do you want me to shoot it or just try to scare it off with some noise?"

"Don't hurt it," I said, "it's just a little one this time!"

I watched the bear from the window as Bruce snuck out. His intention was to shoot into the ground with the little .410 shotgun to scare it off. When I heard the shot, I watched the bear's reaction. She looked up, seemed mildly alarmed, and then dived back into the bin.

Why did he shoot over there so far from it? He should have at least come around to the same side of the house, I thought.

Then a massive, black, hairy curtain crossed the hillside and stopped. The smaller bear gave up on her buffet and walked up to join it. As she stood beside the big male she was dwarfed by his mass.

At the same moment Bruce came back into the house, looking slightly pale and shaken.

"I thought you said it was a little one—that bear is huge! And he never even blinked when I shot over his head!" he whispered.

It was then that we realized the huge, bad-tempered boar had come back from wherever it had been released, and had picked up a mate along the way to share his territory. We watched through the window as he put his paw on her head and sniffed her face as they stood on the hillside, as if checking if she was okay.

"That does it," Bruce said. "I'm using the rubber bullets in the 12 gauge. I want to teach him a lesson. I'm afraid if I don't do something now when I have a chance, he will do some real damage here." He was worried about me, since I'm often alone and outside at all hours of the morning and night.

I armed myself with the .410 shotgun, loaded with real slugs in case we needed them, and followed Bruce up the hill. I kept a wary eye on the bears as they weaved their way through the underbrush. They were either too preoccupied with each other and their search for food to notice us, or they were just totally unafraid. They would pause at each structure they encountered, ripping my precious, hard-earned rehabilitation pens apart as they went. They walked up to the greenhouse, where I was housing fledgling passerines in their final training, learning natural food recognition and flight agility before release. I figured the young flickers and robins in the greenhouse could fly circles around the bears, and since they were small and inconspicuous surely the bears would ignore them. I was wrong.

The two bears entered the greenhouse separately through holes they ripped into the screens and plastic, and began their gory ritual. The visual effect that played like a theatre screen on the steamed plastic covering was eerie and demonic. The sun, which was just visible over the hill, lit the greenhouse with a brilliant flare. The enlarged, distorted silhouettes of the bears were projected on the transparent backdrop of the greenhouse walls; their movements exaggerated as they pulled the fluttering passerines out of the air and killed them.

In the meantime, Bruce had made it to the back lawn. I could tell he could see the bears, but he seemed to be having a hard time trying to aim.

The distorted shapes of backlit bears behind the plastic veil of the greenhouse walls did not make good targets. Then suddenly, the grotesque images of the bears exited out of holes ripped in the backside of the greenhouse and disappeared into the thick woods.

Bruce and I stood on the hill in stunned silence, watching and listening for further indication that they were still around. When we were convinced they had finally left, we approached the damaged greenhouse. I stooped to pick up the crushed little bodies of the birds, choking back tears as I remembered how the poor little things had struggled to survive through the stages from naked nestlings to fully fledged juveniles. I thought of the hours and hours of hand-feeding each species its specific natural diet. I thought of the hours spent capturing the insects and bugs in the huge quantities required by the fast-growing fledglings. I swore then and there that if I was once again presented with the opportunity to destroy that bear, I wouldn't hesitate to take drastic action.

It may sound as if I have an extreme dislike for bears. Not so, as there has only been that one boar that really bothered me. But I do have a healthy respect for their size and unpredictable nature.

Actually, that's an incorrect statement. Their nature is very predictable … for bears!

They know instinctively that as summer wears on, they must gain weight as quickly, easily, and completely as they can. Any and all food is fair forage, but in particular they want fatty foods or foods they can consume in huge quantities. People believe bears are starving when they move into towns to feed, but to the bears as fall approaches no amount of food is enough. And there are no holds barred when it comes to hyperphagia.

There is a common misconception that a failed blueberry crop means the starvation and death of all bears. Blueberries are indeed a very important part of their diet, but bears have adapted to the berry's fickle cycles and do well with other natural foods. For example, calorie for calorie, the beaked hazel nut likely has more to offer than blueberries and is often found in great abundance. We may not notice these important mast foods when we walk in the woods. They grow in an impenetrable twiggy nightmare with their pale green husks blending well with the hue of the leaves. Chipmunks and squirrels collect these nuts as quickly as they ripen, and hoard them in middens for future use. The bears use their incredible nose to scent out the piles. It's more efficient to eat a pre-picked and husked stockpile of beaked hazel than to search for and pick them one at a time.

In forests where there have been major forest tent caterpillar infestations, virtually no blueberry bushes are left after the "worms" have plodded through. Bears must travel to the outskirts of the infestations to find patches to feed on. And blueberry plants require second-year growth to produce fruit. As a result, there are few berries on bushes the year after a major defoliation. But two years after the caterpillars have finally gone, the berry crops can be extraordinary. With all the caterpillar droppings for fertilizer, and the temporary removal of the canopy of leaves allowing sunlight to reach the forest floor, many species of berry plants and fruit bearing shrubs actually flourish after a caterpillar invasion.

In many areas, including my community, bears wander into town in large numbers during their seasonal search for food. Too many of them are conditioned to find human food and in our local situation many bears, I think, still have memories of a recently closed household garbage dumpsite, where their once-constant source of food has been removed. And despite the preponderance of bears in town, some restaurants still leave their grease bins open and unprotected. Late at night, and sometimes even in broad daylight, bears can be seen scooping this disgusting goop into their mouths with great gusto. And in too many cases, a fed bear is a dead bear.

When we drive past the "Fast Food Alley" in Kenora around supper hour, the scent that comes out of grill vents from these restaurants is quite remarkable. Bears with their acute sense of smell must be euphoric when they catch these odours on the wind. And unfortunately, without requirements in place for these outlets to fence in their grease and garbage bins, nuisance bears will continue to wander into town, feed, frighten citizens, and then be destroyed within the city limits.

A few years ago, the Ministry of Natural Resources privatized the service of removing nuisance bears from outside the city limits, contracting it out to private entrepreneurs. But few people in rural areas were willing or financially able to pay the costs for live trapping and removal of the multitudes of bears that decided to damage to their property. A rather flippant but accurate response I have heard is, "Bullets are cheaper!" Of course, this comment came from someone who hadn't yet had to remove a dead, bloated bear from his or her yard in the heat of the summer.

I have had more requests to take in bear cubs in the last few years than in all my previous years of rehabilitation. In most cases, the mothers were shot as nuisances. If the cubs are very small, that is, less than four months of age, I may agree to take them long enough to stabilize their condition and ship them to a rehabilitator who specializes in orphan bears. I will not attempt to raise cubs myself. Even by the end of May, when they are four to five months old, bear cubs are very strong, and I hesitate to fly them off to the more suited rehabilitator, fearing for the safety of airport personnel.

Two little cubs that did meet my reluctant criteria for intervention came to me early one March, and were brought in by ice-fishermen. It seems that, while fishing on Lake of the Woods, these anglers had built a campfire in amongst a pile of uprooted trees on the shoreline. A sow bear, denned up in a nearby tangle of downed trees, was awakened from her hibernation and driven out by the smoke from the fire. Curious, the anglers investigated the den and found three tiny cubs.

What a great opportunity for wildlife photography! they thought.

Apparently, these folks had watched enough documentaries where the cubs were taken out and handled, then put back with the mom without harm. Surely, if they were careful, they could do the same. They didn't realize that when researchers are handling the cubs, the mother remains sleeping in the den. However, this was not the case here, as the sow had run off and left the cubs in the den. This sow would have borne her cubs while she slept, and wouldn't even be aware of their existence; she, therefore, would not have felt the need to protect them. After being kept away from her den for so long, she likely gave up and stumbled off in a sleepy stupor to find another place to sleep.

After the sportsmen had photographed their fill, they returned the cubs to the den. Later, finished fishing for the day, they kicked snow over the campfire, packed up, and left. One fellow, though, had an uneasy feeling about what had happened and checked on the cubs the next day. There was no sign at all that the sow had returned, and by then, one cub had frozen to death. He bundled the remaining two up as warmly as he could and brought them to me.

I finally agreed to take the cubs, at least long enough to find a Wildlife Custodian licensed to raise them. I fed, warmed, and tended to them for a few days until I was sure they had stabilized and were strong enough to make the long flight ahead. The plane the bears flew was "The Bear," with the staff of the local airlines doing everything they could to ensure the little ones remained warm and cozy until they reached their destination. A bear specialist in North Bay who manages Bear With Us willingly received them. The fellow does amazing things with orphan bear cubs and is quite successful in getting them back out into the wild, so I knew they were in good hands.

As I tended to the cute, tiny, perfect bear cubs my heart, hardened by the nasty boar the previous summer, softened somewhat. Bears don't start off their life being destructive. The problems are two-sided, and occur when human and bear worlds collide. Our property is on the fringe of human occupation and boreal forest, so we get bears from both worlds crossing our paths. The wild bears, for the most part, are shy except for the occasional large male that becomes a predator, feeding on calf moose, fawns, and even their own cubs. The town bears are all too familiar with human food and its sources, often encouraged by people who actually think it's okay to feed the bears that come to their yards. More often, though, some bears seem to be able to pattern the town garbage pickup days and raid the bags left on sidewalks. This easy food source reinforces their willingness to remain in close contact with humans. It is likely the bear we had the problems with had become familiar with the human side of life, but had reached the body mass to be a successful predator as well. This ended up being a dangerous and scary combination.

# Feathered and Furred Follies

When I reflect on how creatures like P'silla the porcupine, Cameron the beaver, and the bear cubs came into my life, all too often it is a result of human interference. Although I do get calls from potential rescuers who want to intervene in predator-prey interaction, in these cases I tell the caller not to interfere. If an animal is being pursued or attacked by a natural predator (other than a cat, dog, or child), I believe that we should not interfere. One example is a baby otter saved from the claws of an eagle. It must have given the rescuer an initial feeling of benevolence, but the victim could not survive its wounds. The eagle, deprived of her meal, likely sought out a littermate to replace her stolen dinner. It's a very difficult decision to make when the life to be saved is so innocent and young, but sometimes we have to let these events unfold as they do when we are not around to witness them.

I once had a call asking me to take over the care of an adult deer that had been rescued from a pack of wolves. Somewhat apprehensively, I agreed to help. It wasn't a pretty sight. I could see the deer was horribly mangled and would never recover from shock or its injuries. It would have been a more humane and expedient death had they left the deer to succumb to the hungry predators. His stress and pain only increased as two-legged rescuers, although well-meaning, pulled and pushed on his broken body to load him onto a sled. His great heart finally burst from fear and pain. I knew the wolves, deprived of their hard-earned meal, would now be forced to kill another deer to feed the pack, and the flesh of the one that was rescued ended up out of the available food chain, likely in a covered landfill, where not even scavengers could benefit from its death.

Most folks who have observed the beauty of nature as well as its ferocity seem to know when to interfere and when not to. An injured prey species left for a predator to finish off has served a purpose. If that same little victim is saved from the predator, only to be euthanized with chemicals to stop its pain, it has served no purpose. Its chemical-ridden flesh can feed no one, rendering its death meaningless. It's not just humans and natural predators that cause injuries. Human technology and how wildlife responds to it may bring some injured animal to my care. Animals and birds often put themselves into dangerous predicaments, mostly because of bad judgment and youthful inexperience. A common plight is the one of young loons during migration in the late fall. Adult loons migrate in late summer or early fall, leaving behind the young loons. These juveniles gather in large flocks, feeding and gaining strength until around late November, when the big lakes start to freeze over. Once freeze-up starts, the young birds will start their journey. Some of the northern-born young may become exhausted during their first long migration flight or perhaps encounter bad weather as they leave for the south. They require large expanses of open water to land on and take off from, and if forced down due to bad weather and snow squalls, sometimes misinterpret what they see below them.

I have had several young loons brought in to me who have mistaken bare, wet highways for rivers after the first snows of the fall. The loon's landing impact injuries are often severe, and may be exacerbated by vehicles colliding with or running over the downed birds. Others suffer scraped keels and beak injuries, which may or may not be repairable. Loons' legs are adapted for swimming, not for bearing their body weight, and so cannot be kept easily in captivity while wounds heal. If I can do a quick epoxy patch job on a beak or sew together a bit of torn skin and release them to be on their way the same day, all the better. The less handled the better, especially since they are such unwilling patients, and are always looking for the chance to bury their beak in your eyeball.

It seems the birds that are born and spend most of their life in the north learn the hardest lessons when forced south, where they encounter human development and motor vehicles for the first time. Great grey owls have cyclical invasions, as do the other species of northern owl, when the red vole or lemming populations in their northern habitat decline. Hundreds of these impressive birds will line up along roads and highways seeking food. This ancient species has no fear of humans or domestic pets. They do not seem to recognize them as threats.

They also do not understand the danger of motor vehicles. Whether the roadways resemble vole-saturated riverbanks from their home territory, or whether mice and voles flock to the highways for discarded food and accumulated road salt, no one really knows, but the number of these magnificent birds killed along highways is incredibly high. My theory is that these birds sometimes see chunks of snow and what might be called "fender bergs" fall off vehicles and bounce along the surface of the roadway; they mistake them for mice.

I was driving home one day and was barely able to stop in time to avoid running into a grey shadow that had suddenly crossed the road behind the vehicle directly in front of me. The shadow landed on a brown chunk of snow that had spun off the fender of the vehicle I was following. Had I not been driving slowly, or had there been a vehicle close behind, I would likely have hit the beautiful bird. While great greys look massive and stand close to a metre high, their body is actually quite small, not much more than the size of a ruffed grouse under all that feathering.

I couldn't believe a report I once heard on our national news channel. In a story about a great grey owl eruption the anchor who said, "These massive birds have been known to take cats…" The great greys have weak talons designed for taking small voles, lemmings, mice, and only very occasionally squirrels or young rabbits. But since an adult great grey usually weighs less than two pounds, they do not and physically cannot take cats. Great horned owls on the other hand may take out a cat, but it's extremely unlikely a great grey could. Unfortunately, this erroneous broadcast probably made the great grey an enemy of at least a few cat lovers.

Wild animals injure themselves in other more familiar ways. One such indignity results when flocks of waxwings, particularly Bohemian waxwings, indulge in consumption of fermenting fruits like crab apples, plums, or blueberries in the late fall and winter. Drunk as proverbial sailors, some fall onto the ground and if not rescued and warmed can and do die of exposure. This is one of the natural predicaments in which I will interfere. Many rehabbers and other kind souls have saved the lives of waxwings by providing them a safe place to sleep it off. Fortunately, these drunks usually only need a night of rest and a long drink of water and can be set free the next day.

Then there are the mishaps that are common tragedies or freak accidents. In such instances, the potential for rescue is low. Bruce called to me from the driveway one cold snowy morning to show me something. When I walked outside he pointed to Brill, who was looking proud with a limp grouse in her mouth. We assumed it had hit a window and fallen to the ground, where Brill had found it after having picked up the scent. Funny, though, no window showed the inevitable smudge of feather dust that a bird's body makes when it hits the glass hard. Then I looked up, and in the snow on the roof I could make out the marks where it had hit the roof at top speed. His last act on this earth was to leave a grouse's version of a snow angel, a flop, flop, flop all the way down the slope of the roof, over the gutter and onto the ground. There is something to be said for survival of the fittest (or smartest).

There was a time when, I must admit, my actions almost contradicted the mantra of healers of all kinds: above all, do no harm. The patient was a permanently damaged but otherwise healthy white pelican I had received and treated. I was preparing it for shipment to the Assiniboine Zoo in Winnipeg, Manitoba. Any specimens going to a zoo facility must be disease- and parasite-free, so I was giving it a final check to make sure that the medicine had worked and its infestations of throat lice were gone. As usual, I was working alone.

When threatened, pelicans put up a lot of huff and bluff, with loud clapping of their bills and false charges and lunges. Even Cameron had learned this, in an earlier encounter with this same bird. I have found that as long as I avoid the hook on the end of the bill, the rest of the appendage can do little damage. So when this particular bird behaved as pelicans are wont to, I let him clap onto my hand and held him firmly against my side, while I shone a small penlight down his throat. I was looking for attached flukes that may have survived treatment. Satisfied none remained, I backed to a safe distance and released his beak. But as soon as I did so, he lunged at me and the penlight flew out of my hands and onto the floor. We both dived for it, but he won.

I watched in horror as the penlight, still lit, swirled around in his beak and down the hatch. Its beam was still visible through the thin membrane of his pouch and I watched as it slowly slipped down, down, down his long neck until it disappeared into the thicker feathers of his breast. He proudly walked back into his enclosure, seemingly unaware of his newly acquired inner glow.

Oh, blast! I thought. He's supposed to be shipped early the next morning so what do I do now? I can't send him off with a foreign object in him.

Fortunately, like many water-birds, pelicans regurgitate their last meal when scared or annoyed, likely as an adaptation to lighten the load for quick flight. Counting on this, I held on to a slim hope I would be able to retrieve my light.

"Booo!" I yelled. "Booo!" He clapped his beak at my head.

Encouraged by his reaction, I opened the enclosure door and forced him to walk out. "Booo!" With that, he held his head down and started shaking his open beak.

Great! I thought. He's going to chuck!

"Booo!" Yes! I could see a small glow: up, up, up, until like a drunken fire-fly it swirled around in the pouch membranes. Then, with one final, mighty shake, he hurled it across the floor, along with his partly digested last meal.

Well, they hadn't said he couldn't have a *light* lunch before I shipped him.

# Demeter's Grief

By mid-September, Persephone looked like a perfectly proportioned white-tailed deer, only in miniature. A PocketPolly Persephone, so to speak. Her spots could now be wiped off with a gloved hand and the grey, hollow hair of her winter coat had started to replace the fine, reddish fawn hair. The wild deer were spending more time in our fields, feeding on the frost-touched clovers, and tracks in the soft clay were evidence she was joining them regularly, occasionally wandering with them a half a kilometre or more from the house. When I would call for her at her mealtime, it took longer and longer for her to come in. Most fawns would have been weaned by now, but I felt that she needed the extra nutrition to help her through a long winter.

After one particular feeding I prepared myself to sit in the field with her, intent on finishing my novel while she browsed, only to see her focus and stare into the nearby woods. Ears tilted far forward, tail twitching, with a little nasal "nee-ew," she stotted up the deer trail and into the bushes. Blows and whistles from adult deer announced she had made contact. Sighing happily, I gathered up my belongings and headed back to the house. I was no longer needed in her life, I thought, and that was a good thing.

The adult deer became more nervous once the hunting season opened in October. They still came around, but mostly under cover of darkness. Up to the end of September the weather had been mild with only an occasional light night frost, allowing the fawn continued access to nutritive, actively growing browse. Along with the occasional bottle of goat's milk, she received a few handfuls of deer pellet. Apples were a favourite treat as well. I felt safe leaving a pile of food at the edge of the field for her, as it appeared now the bears had become less active.

I wasn't too worried about her being shot by a deer hunter, as she was so tiny. I was fairly sure no self-respecting hunter would forfeit his or her deer tag on such a diminutive specimen. However, I elected to wear fluorescent orange even though our land was posted, just to be sure a poacher didn't mistake me for game. I worried that after seeing me in this protective garb, Persephone might come to believe humans in orange were her friends. I could only hope this wouldn't happen.

One especially cold, crisp evening in late October I was feeding Persephone down by the partly frozen beaver pond, aware I was in drab attire but too intent on getting the chores done to put on my blaze orange clothing. Cameron the beaver was busy opening up a canal in the newly forming frazil ice to get to his feeding spot, where he was sure an apple or bread bun awaited him. I was off in thought waiting for Persephone to drain her bottle when suddenly there was a deafening roar and crack. Sedges in front of me exploded into the air! Fragments of ice and grasses went spinning across the smooth ice of the pond and crashing into the shore. In an instant, Persephone was gone, disappearing up the hill into thick brush, blowing and snorting her fear.

My first thought was that either Persephone or I had been shot at. So I yelled (swore, actually!) to announce that I was human to the unseen assailant. But there was only silence except for Cameron's happy whine as he reached his goodies along the shore. Cameron, surprisingly, was not disturbed at all. After a few moments he went back to breaking ice, and it was only then that I realized what had happened. Cameron was breaking and moving large chunks of thin fresh ice and hurling them up onto the thicker, older and smooth black ice, which rimmed the edge of the pond. He put enough muscle behind these slabs to send them like a curling rock, whup, whup, whup, across the ice until they sliced into the brittle dried sedges, chopping them off in a spray of chaff, exploding the ice into bits, and making a loud retort like a gunshot. So that was it! A beaver's version of curling. How Canadian.

By the end of October Persephone's coat was thick and fluffy. The first significant amounts of snow fell and stayed on the ground. I had noticed that, as the nights became colder, and colder she became increasingly agitated. Uncharacteristically, the leaves clung tenaciously to their branches that year, providing her and other animals some protection from the biting wind. But on really windy nights, she was forced further into the woods to bed than had been her habit, in areas where there were a few small groves of spruce. These sheltered areas provided her with windbreak and warmth. During the day she seemed needy and confused, often following me as I did my chores. This was not a good thing and surprised me, as she had been so independent before. It was as if she wanted me to lead her somewhere. I guess it made sense, as the other deer were moving out of their summer range into thicker cover and to peninsulas on the unfrozen big lakes and rivers, benefiting from the moderating factors of the open water. The bucks that roamed our fields also made her nervous, as they chased does and even approached her, despite her youth. Strong musky smells that lingered in the air around their scrapes and rubs made her snort a danger call when she encountered them.

One blustery night she followed me into the henhouse when I fed the chickens, then down the hill, where I fed the rabbits. I gave her deer pellets to eat, thinking she was hungry, but these she ignored, squinting at me through half-closed eyes as falling snowflakes clung to her eyelids. She had her ears back and chin tilted up, body language she used when angry or sulking. After staring at me for a while, she blended back into the mass of blown-down trees behind the henhouse, browsing, sniffing the air, hoof held suspended before the next tentative step ... very nervous. I felt I should have stayed with her while she browsed, but I was fighting the flu and wanted to be back inside the house, where it was warm.

After a feverish night's sleep, with the dogs barking and whining at some unknown foe, I allowed myself to sleep in. The flu had taken a firm hold over me during the night and when dawn came I felt horrible. Instead of rising at an early hour and feeding Persephone and the rest of the critters as I usually would have, I stumbled out of bed late. It was well past eight when I finally prepared her food and by then, it had already been light for some time. The dogs were still growling on occasion, which led me to assume they could smell or hear Persephone walking around the yard, looking for me or browsing on the frost-tipped clovers, as she was wont to do. When I walked to the field and called for her, I noted that there were no deer tracks in the fresh snow that had fallen during the night.

Odd, I thought. She should have been wandering around by now.

I called for her, first by mouth. But when there was no response and my sore throat squeaked and croaked, I switched to my store-bought doe call. Still no luck. I had a sinking feeling. Even though Persephone had often refused to come to me on windy days, this seemed different, more ominous. For one, the wind was light. I decided to turn my attentions to other matters and tended to my other wild and domestic critters, all the while keeping an eye out for any sign of her. But there was none.

My other chores completed, I decided to try again to find her. I warmed up her food and then walked back to the field, expecting at any moment to see her bouncing out of the bushes to greet me. Still no sign, but a shadow in the rising sun caught my eye.

A raven? Not too surprising, as I knew the ravens flew over the field all the time on their way to or from their rookery, or making a pass by the big hill where I often leave food for the eagles. No sooner had that thought run through my brain when I spotted an eagle, circling low over me. But as I watched I realized none of the birds were circling the food pile, they were focused on our path leading to the big hill. As I watched, both the eagle and a raven dropped down into the trees. Oh no!

I ran back to the house. Old Heidi was already waiting at the door as if she expected me, barking her excitement.

"Sorry, old girl, I have to be able to move fast this time."

I knew Heidi would be much better at scenting out what I feared I would find, but with her age and the cold, damp weather she was just too stiff and sore to accompany me on my search. I would need to test Brill's hunting abilities this time.

"Come Brill! You'll have to do this solo." I grabbed a single-shot .22 and a handful of shells. Although she obeyed my command, Brill did not share Heidi's enthusiasm for the impending hunt. With apprehension in her eyes, she obediently followed me out the door and across the field.

A short way up the trail I encountered tracks of several running deer, hoof prints gouged deep into the soft mud and skiff of snow, showing how they

had been running, slipping, and sliding on the greasy trail. Persephone's tiny hooves were evident among them. I hoped what I saw was just the tracks of bucks chasing does, with Persephone caught up in the excitement. But then there were other tracks, obviously canine in origin, and they weren't from my dogs. The sound of ravens nearby alarmed me.

I told Brill, "Search," and immediately she swung her head up, sniffed the air, growled, and began searching. A flash of black and the flapping of wings from a nearby poplar startled me, but it also told me our search would be a short one. Moments later, Brill was growling and barking furiously into the bushes and then she raced up to the top of a small rocky knob. There she barked to indicate she had found her prey.

There was so little left of the Lilliputian fawn that, although tiny, had completely filled and enriched my summer days. A small patch of fur, complete with the miniature tail she used to flag so proudly, a tiny section of jawbone, and a small mound of paunch contents lay in the flattened lichen on the edge of a rock ledge. Small curds of goat's milk, interspersed with the lichens and twigs she had consumed the previous evening, lay in a pile, spurned by the pack of carnivores that had taken her life. The ground itself was only slightly disturbed, as if her death had been quick and efficient. Then my eyes, brimming with tears, caught a flash of colour in the snow-encrusted limbs above. Brilliant flecks of red gleamed in the sun, high in the birch and poplars, tossed with such force they stuck to the highest limbs, testament to the viciousness of Persephone's attackers. My body cringed as I imagined the scene.

A crack and crash nearby and Brill's anxious whine brought me back to the present. I felt a shiver up my spine as if I were being watched. The wolves must still be nearby. The .22 calibre I carried was puny protection if the pack decided they wanted Brill for dessert. I called Brill to me and then fought tears all the way back home, with both Brill and I sending furtive glances over our shoulders at every rustle.

The next day when I forced myself to return to the site of the kill, I saw that the wolves had returned for a final check, rolling on Persephone's miniscule remnants as if to absorb her final essence into their bodies. They must have been waiting and watching as Brill and I left. Evidence in the snow showed they had bedded near the kill site in the thick cover where I had heard noises the day before. I backtracked the running deer tracks to where the chase had begun, seeing how the wolves had snuck along the top of a rock ridge, which overlooked a small gully where two or three adult deer had bedded down in the thick blow-down after feeding. A tiny bed and fawn tracks in amongst the adults' indicated that Persephone had sought company after leaving me on that fateful evening and had been with the wild deer when the attack took place. Her tiny legs and body size were no match for the large timber wolves that took her down. The other deer had been able to outrun their attackers.

Feeling helpless and knowing there was nothing I could do, I left Persephone's remains and began to cross the field, heading back towards the house. Both my feet and my heart felt heavy and I could feel the harsh bitterness of winter in the wind, a sure sign of the mythological Demeter's grief at the loss of her Persephone.

For me, raising wild animals for release to the wild is an emotional roller coaster. My intentions are to raise them to a stage where they have an equal chance of living the life of a youngster raised in the wild. Whether this fawn had been raised by me or by its mom, its tiny size would have made it susceptible to all canids—fox, coyote, and timber wolf. But still I felt guilty. Had I gone to feed her at the normal time that morning, instead of giving in to my flu symptoms and the comforts of my bed, could I have stopped the kill? Or would the wolves have confronted me? My mind roiled with anguish. It was little comfort when I finally convinced myself that even if I could have saved her this time, the wolves would have come back again and again. In all likelihood, her fate was inevitable.

Thinking back on the events before her demise, I realized that the nervousness Persephone felt the previous night had likely been from the smell of the wolves in the wind. The presence of the wolves also explained why the dogs had been growling during the night.

As sad as I was that her life had ended so unfulfilled and so violently, I eventually accepted that it disturbed me less to lose her to wolves than if it had been to a human act. Had a hunter shot her on our property, or if she'd been hit on our road by local speedsters, or had been taken down by uncontrolled neighbourhood dogs, I would not have accepted her death as easily. But here on the northern limits of deer range, white-tailed deer populations have always survived by naturally selecting the larger-bodied and strongest animals. Tiny specimens like Persephone would only survive the gentlest of winters. These small-bodied animals are the first to be preyed upon, and the first to succumb to deep snow and bone-chilling cold, leaving the stronger, larger fawns to continue their genetic line.

But somehow, these hard biological facts don't make up for the loss of a soft, small, brown-and-white fawn.

As the ides of March approached, I could almost believe that Demeter had truly influenced our winter in her grief. Although temperatures had been mild and there had been relatively little snow until the end of October, the weather had then turned bleak and blustery. While the major snowfalls had held off until January, the cold and wind had not. Leaves which had not had time to dry and die had been quick-frozen, and their brown and leathery remains still clung to branches, defying even the strongest winds. February too was colder than normal. By March, the normal hints of thaw on southern slopes were still absent. I concluded that if it weren't Demeter's grief that determined this weather then it must be a fickle northwestern Ontario winter … they have commonalities.

# Another Sad Farewell

The winter had been slow for receiving patients. There were none of the normal owl eruptions with the resultant car collisions and the eagles, always foraging on roadkill, had been able to dodge oncoming vehicles. For once, I had no wild patients requiring special care and attention. For this respite I was grateful.

This meant I had time to tend to our ailing, geriatric Heidi. During Christmas she had showed a brief period of renewed energy and a puppy-like eagerness which surprised and delighted us. She once again climbed stairways that for at least a couple of years had been too difficult for her. With a blissful, dreamy look in her eyes she eagerly accompanied Bruce, Brill, and me on the long walks to her favourite lookout on the big hill, sniffing the winds that blew up from the valley. The truck rides to Grandma's were ever a favourite for her. She seemed to have found a new *joie de vivre*.

Then, just as suddenly, she started to melt away before our eyes. I switched her to softened food, thinking perhaps her teeth and gums were bothering her, but to no avail. Her weight continued to drop, and lethargy set in.

Dr. Celia broke the news in her kind and gentle way of the cancer that had developed. We spoke of possibilities and decided surgery was not an option. It seemed the right thing for us was to maintain palliative care, with Celia's acupuncture treatments reducing the pain of the spreading cancer and the wonders of herbal medicine maintaining her in comfort and with dignity intact.

Bruce was required to use up some overtime from work, which was opportune. He was able to come home and help me care for her, and his presence cheered up both Heidi and me immensely. We comforted our old dog as best we could, giving in to her whims and special needs to be carried about and catered to. Although she maintained her ability to walk until near the end, the slippery kitchen floors were her downfall. Her feet had lost their fatty, soft padding and could no longer grip the smooth surface. I bought her little socks that toddlers often wear, complete with little rubber paw tracks on the soles, and with these she maintained some level of mobility. But this too passed.

As we took turns comforting her we would remember how she had filled our life with joy.

"Remember the night when you fell asleep after putting her outside?" Bruce grinned. It had happened years earlier, when Heidi had been in heat. We made a point of keeping close tabs on her when she was in this state, as we didn't want puppies, especially from an unknown sire. However, too many sleepless nights with the neighbourhood's gigolos barking at the door had exhausted me, and after putting her out for her toilet, I had been unable to stay awake. Having dozed off, I woke with a start to a lot of barking and whining going on outside. Bruce and I both rushed out, only to see a pack of her suitors disappear into the darkness. Heidi stood there with a silly grin on her face and her face covered in slobbers.

"How long was she out? Do you think anything happened? You were supposed to watch over her when you put her out!"

"I don't know, Bruce. I fell asleep, but I'm sure nothing happened ... I hope...."

Heidi, as if in answer to our question, walked past my open purse, grabbed my cigarettes (I smoked back then) and leaped onto the bed with the pack in her mouth. We stared at each other in disbelief.

"Oh no! The proverbial cigarette...." we said in unison.

Sadly, she never did become a mother.

"Hey, Bruce, how about the time you and your editor went grouse hunting with her? Gary hadn't believed you about what a super little hunting dog she was until he witnessed it himself." I remembered sitting at the supper table while Bruce's editor regaled us with the story of Heidi's hunting prowess. Seems that after an afternoon of unproductive grouse hunting, they finally lucked out and saw a few on the road ahead. Gary took first shot and felled a grouse, and then a second bird took to the air, which Bruce promptly felled. As the second bird fell to the ground Heidi flushed a third grouse, which she rushed at. Barking furiously, Heidi made a couple of bounds, sailed into the air, and grabbed the flying grouse with her mouth. Another bound, and she delivered the live and unharmed grouse to Bruce's hand.

Heidi also had the amazing ability to spit. I first noticed this un-dog-like trait while she was still a pup cutting her adult teeth. I had been playfully ruffling her hair when, caught up in the game, she grabbed my hand a little too roughly. As her needle-sharp puppy teeth raked my flesh, I pulled my hand back quickly, pulling out a loose canine tooth. Afraid I had hurt her, I made a big fuss over her, showing her the tooth and generally being a silly human being, trying to show I had meant her no harm. She looked at the extracted tooth, looked at me quizzically, and then went back to doing doggy things.

Later that day I was sitting on the couch reading as she chewed on her toy bone nearby. I heard a little squeal, and when I looked up she was sitting in front of me with a strange expression. There appeared to be something in her mouth. For some reason her look told me that she had something for me so I held out my hand. "Ptewww"—she spit another canine tooth into my hand, feverishly wagging her tail, obviously looking for more attention and baby talk.

She used this spitting talent many times, usually after coming to me with the "guess what I got" look. When I held out my hand, I could be surprised with anything from a dried-up frog to an indignant baby turtle, a bone that needed the marrow scooped out for her or maybe something even more disgusting.

The bone-and-marrow thing got a little out of hand, I think. I had indulged her shamelessly when she was young. When I saw her frantically trying to gnaw the last little bit of marrow out of her new meat bone to the point that her lips and gums bled, I felt sorry for her and commanded her, "Give,

Mom fix." It only took her a few times to realize that if she gave me her bone, I could be trusted to give it back with the marrow conveniently scooped out so she could reach it. After that, "Mom fix" could be anything from a stolen lunch bag that she wanted the sandwich from to a live mouse stuck in a bottle. When bones were not to be had she devised her own amusement. The curious dog soon de-squeaked her squeaky plastic worm toy. This was the only toy Heidi ever destroyed, but it was for a purpose. It was as if she realized the small hole in the end would nicely hold kibble or cookies. When she was bored, she would bring the toy to me and I would fill it with dry dog food for her to patiently remove, one piece at a time. I spoiled her rotten.

There were times, though, when I scolded her, then was immediately repentant. Heidi never needed any punishment other than a stern voice.

Once, as I bent over the table doing the distasteful task of writing cheques to cover the ever-growing pile of household bills on my table, Heidi decided a walk would do us both good. The leash was also lying on the table, dropped there after our last walk. Before I realized what she was doing, she had grabbed the leash and pulled it and all the bills and cheques off the table. I watched as the papers slipped and glided under the refrigerator, the stove, and other unreachable corners.

"Heidi, you bad girl! Bruce doesn't pay me enough to look after you! Go!" I watched as she slunk into the bedroom, leaving me to gather my bills and regain my patience.

As I settled back at the table, I heard a chirp beside me. Heidi sat there with the saddest of eyes staring up at me. She held something in her mouth. Feeling my impatience build, I held out my hand, expecting to receive a toy or bone peace offering, when "ptwee"—out popped a ten-dollar bill. I never did figure out where she had found this money, as I was pretty sure I was broke, but it was as if she was offering to pay me for spending time with her. After a quick apologetic hug, we went together for a well-deserved walk.

Bruce, Heidi, and I had many exciting trips and adventures together. She loved camping but couldn't sleep at night unless we left a radio playing softly. It seemed the cacophony of nature was too stimulating, and she would spend the night sniffing and barking into the darkness unless we distracted her. Her anxiety at night was evident one beautiful fall evening while we camped on the edge of a stream. The noises of geese, moose, and beavers were just too scary for young Heidi. When she whimpered to go outside the tent, I opened the

flap for her. The look on her face seemed imploring, so I started to push her out the flap when she whirled and grabbed her teddy bear. When I checked on her a few minutes later, I saw a vision I will always remember when I think of Heidi. There she sat, straight and proud, on the smooth flat rock overlooking the cattail-lined creek, silhouetted in the moonlight, with her thumb-sucking teddy bear positioned right beside her. Life isn't so scary when you have a buddy, I guess.

I know that someday I will have to write about Heidi. She was a rare breed and an uncommon character. Her intelligence was at times unnerving. But for now, her legacy lives on in Bruce's article in *Gun Dog Magazine* (August/September 1994) which is now found on the website www.wachtelhund.org. These dogs are in themselves amazing animals, but Heidi seemed extraordinary.

Bruce and I realized she was slipping fast. We debated whether to take her to our veterinarian for her final sleep, but since she didn't appear to be in uncontrollable pain, we preferred to keep her in familiar surroundings. I knew that her time was near one morning when I prepared to visit my mom. The dogs sensed this trip each weekend and eagerly awaited it but this time she didn't want to come. Instead, she lay back down on her bed and gave a big sigh. I knew then that she was losing awareness of her surroundings. Her eyebrows still followed my movements, but the light in her eyes was fading.

That evening before I started to make supper, I checked on the vaporizer I had set up near her bed to help her breathe. Then I moistened her mouth with a wet sponge, gave her a gentle pat and cuddle, and went back into the kitchen. She turned her head a bit to watch me leave and sighed deeply. As I worked over the stove, something told me she needed me. I called Bruce and we went to her side to give her a final farewell.

Fourteen years to the day from that cold March day we brought her home, we once again patted our beautiful friend's head as she slipped quietly away for her final sleep, her hair still silky and her dignity intact.

Saying goodbye to old friends is so hard. Even saying goodbye to the little wild lives that are too fragile to live, and whom I know only briefly, is hard to bear. But despite the emotional roller coasters there is always, according to mythology, Persephone's footfall returning with the seeds of spring. This promise of flowers and beauty for at least another short period of time keeps making it all worthwhile.

Maybe it's this promise that gives all of us living in these northern climes hope and determination. In a way it is like when the weatherman gives a depressing long-range forecast of cold temperatures and dreary skies but subtly slips in a mild and sunny prediction at the tail end. We know there is a good chance it won't really be mild on that last day, but it gives us the fortitude to brave a bout of miserable northern weather, and look forward to that warm day that will eventually come.

It was cold and wet, but the smell of spring was definitely in the air as I walked up to the field and stood beside a fresh mound of earth facing the beaver pond. As I arranged a small solar lantern near the head of the mound, a brown-and-white-streak raced by me.

"Slow down and pay your respects, Brill," I murmured.

In response to my voice, Brill walked over and looked quizzically at me. She sniffed tentatively at the fresh earth before staring down at it and whimpering softly with her tail beating in a "tip tip tip" greeting for the old friend settled deep within.

"Okay, let's go back," I sniffed, as I gave Heidi's grave a final pat.

Battling the sleet and icy wind, I walked down towards the beaver pond. Brill was already on top of Cameron's lodge, pulling at a still frozen stick. Suddenly a splash and dark disturbance in the snow and ice of the pond caught my attention. Cameron had survived the winter and had now opened a hole in his icy domain, braving the cold, to hiss his displeasure at Brill. He waddled past the startled dog and snatched a fresh aspen from the hillside, before grumbling back into the watery darkness.

Brill growled and stared in the direction of the upper pond. I glanced up nervously, remembering the bear from the previous year. Surely it was too early in the spring for him to be moving around? Then the object of Brill's attention came into view. A pair of otters suddenly appeared, popping in and out of the thawing beaver dam. As they ran across the ice, their sleek tilde-shaped bodies gleamed despite the low light. In the distant skies a large flock of sandhill cranes sounded their confusion, arguing over which way to fly. The flocks of migrating Canada geese wouldn't be far behind, I thought, and hopefully with them a pair of familiar webs would be landing on our pond again. All of these were sure signs of spring. Demeter must have her Persephone back. And with these seeds of spring there will be more little orphans that I— hopefully—will be able to do my part to release back out to where they belong: more moose calves, more fawns, more goslings. But hopefully, no more bears...